THE WHISTLEBLOWER

CONFESSIONS OF A HEALTHCARE HITMAN

THE WHISTLEBLOWER

CONFESSIONS OF A HEALTHCARE HITMAN

by Peter Rost MD

Soft Skull Press   Brooklyn NY

2006

The Whistleblower
©2006 Peter Rost
Cover Design: Peter Garner
Book Design: Luke Gerwe

Soft Skull Press
55 Washington St, STE 804
Brooklyn, NY 11201
Distributed by Publishers Group West
www.pgw.com | 800 788 3123
Printed in Canada

Library of Congress Cataloging-in-Publication Data

Rost, Peter.
The whistleblower : confessions of a healthcare hitman / Peter Rost.
    p. cm.
ISBN-13: 978-1-933368-39-9 (alk. paper)
ISBN-10: 1-933368-39-X (alk. paper)
1. Pfizer Inc.--Management. 2. Pharmacia Corp.--Management. 3. Rost,
Peter. 4. Pharmaceutical industry--Corrupt practices. 5. Pharmaceutical
ethics. 6. Whistle blowing. I. Title.

HD9666.9.P44R67 2006
338.7'6151092--dc22
[B]

2006019069

To
Alexander,
Maximilian,
Sebastian

and

to
Tina

Contents

*"All that is required for evil
to triumph is for good men to
do nothing."*
　　　　　　—*Edmund Burke*

A STUDY OF 233 WHISTLEBLOWERS by Donald Soeken of St. Elizabeth's Hospital in Washington, DC, found that the average whistleblower was a family man in his forties with a strong conscience and high moral values.

After blowing the whistle on fraud, 90 percent of the whistleblowers were fired or demoted, 27 percent faced lawsuits, 26 percent had to seek psychiatric or physical care, 25 percent suffered alcohol abuse, 17 percent lost their homes, 15 percent got divorced, 10 percent attempted suicide, and 8 percent were bankrupted. But in spite of all this, only 16 percent said that they wouldn't blow the whistle again.

Prologue

Saturday, December 31, 2005

"PETER, CAN I TALK TO YOU?" My wife didn't look happy at all. She walked over to the CD player, turned off the music, and sat down next to me on the sofa.

"What is it?"

"I just read your book proposal."

"Oh, so what do you think?" From her hesitation, I could tell something bad was coming.

"I don't *want* to be exposed this way. People we know are going to read this. It's embarrassing."

"But that's what'll make this book interesting."

"They're all going to say 'poor you' to me. I don't want them to know what we've gone through."

"Wait. I'm not sure they're going to say that. This is a David vs. Goliath fight. And we're going to win." I tried to sound convincing.

"But we don't know that yet . . . We don't know anything about the future."

"So what's the risk with this?"

"Everyone with something to hide will be mad at you because of this book. And you might come across as vindictive and vengeful. Maybe even as an opportunist."

"Do you think I am those things?"

"No, I know this is about our survival, but *others* don't know the whole situation. They're not in the middle of it, living this thing day in and day out."

"But don't you think I could write this in the right tone to make sure people understand that I didn't have a choice? And that writing this book is really an act of last resort? I've tried everything, you know."

"It depends—some people might simply view you as a tattletale anyway. But of course, those who agree with you will love this book. And everyone thought you had nothing to gain, but now they'll know that there was something in it for you."

"Like what?"

"You prolonged your employment and you write about how you fought to stop them from firing you."

"Yeah, but Pfizer could've fired me right away when I spoke up. I took a big risk when I did that. I'm taking another big risk with this book."

"I know you are taking a risk, but not everyone else will realize that. They may think this is all very self serving. And just remember, sometimes you've lost. When you tried to warn Pfizer the first time, you didn't know how dangerous it was to speak up."

"Right, but now I'm using that experience to help us survive."

"You don't know that. You don't know what'll happen if this book gets published. Many of those journalists you've gotten to know are going to write about it. And you don't know what they'll say. They may be upset because you didn't tell the whole story from the beginning. People in the drug industry are going to talk about this book. You'll never work again."

"It's not like I'm having a lot of job offers right now. And it's not like I *could* talk about everything that I've written about in this book when I started talking to the press back in 2004. The complaint I filed against Pfizer was sealed by the court, no one was allowed to know, not even Pfizer."

"But many may think that you took advantage of the company. You got paid for doing nothing. Not that you had much of a choice. And people may not understand that. And even if they do, you were a vice president with a lot of power working for an industry many abhor. Your job was to improve profits and to fire people when you had to. You were a healthcare hitman and many may not forgive you for that."

"So do you think *anything* good can come out of this book?"

"It's not like most authors make much money. But perhaps this could lead to something new, some way that we can support ourselves and build a future. But the drug companies aren't going to change how they do business. You're just a tiny mosquito to them; irritating until they squash you, just like you squashed people you didn't think performed well."

"What if we can help legalize reimportation of drugs because of this book?"

"Maybe then there's something good. But honestly, it's just a book, how much could it really achieve? And most of the politicians who fought for reimportation have given up. They used you and then they tossed you away. Plus, that wouldn't make *me* happy. I want to provide for our children. But if you can make this book a success, I guess that's fine."

She had that look in her eyes that I knew so well. She knew that nothing could stop me. And I knew that if I didn't make this work, I'd be in serious trouble.

ONE

Vultures at the Gates

EVERYONE REMEMBERS WHERE THEY WERE when they heard about the terrorist attack of September 11. Most know what they were doing when they first learned about the devastation and flooding after the hurricane in New Orleans. Those who are old enough can still picture the moment when they saw the first man walk on the moon. Those were all life-altering events to a generation of people. Few people, however, will remember when the drug company Pharmacia disappeared. That is, except for the people working for this pharmaceutical corporation. For them, a day in July 2002 became etched in their minds more clearly than any of the events described above when they discovered that Pfizer would take over their company.

I was far away from Pharmacia's New Jersey headquarters—on another continent—when I learned that we were being bought by Pfizer. As a vice president of marketing at Pharmacia I was responsible not only for U.S. marketing of Genotropin, a human growth hormone, but also for global marketing of the same product. Sales of Genotropin were expected to top $600 million around the world, making ours one of the largest franchises within Pharmacia. In addition to my U.S. marketing staff, I also had a research group located in Sweden reporting to me. My work that summer in 2002 had taken me back to my native country and its capital city, Stockholm.

I was in a pretty good mood. I had decided that I had enough information to make a definitive recommendation to management to kill a new database system that had occupied my research group for three years.

I celebrated by taking one of the blue Stockholm buses, part of an elaborate and gleaming public-transportation system, to a green cape ten minutes away from downtown Stockholm. I sat down on an old, wooden jetty and watched an armada of sailboats and motorboats enter the Stockholm archipelago. The sharp northern sun warmed my skin and the waterway before me resembled a motorway, thick with recreational traffic.

I checked my watch. Although midday in Stockholm, it was barely morning in New Jersey. I dialed the office number on my cell phone to retrieve my voicemail messages.

The Surprise

The first message was from our CEO, Fred Hassan. Such a voicemail wasn't unusual in and of itself. Fred was an avid communicator, and he regularly sent voicemails and e-mails to all employees, telling us about the business and how we were doing. He was thought of by Pharmacia employees as one of the few enlightened leaders in the pharmaceutical industry. He also had an excellent reputation outside of Pharmacia, a company that Fred had saved when he became CEO back in 1997.

Back then it had been so bad that one analyst wrote, "Only a miracle can save this company."[1] A couple of years later, Fred had moved Pharmacia's headquarters from London to New Jersey, and consummated a dramatic, $37 billion merger with Monsanto.[2] The deal gave him Celebrex, a pain and arthritis drug for which Monsanto had signed a co-promotion deal with Pfizer, which meant that both companies would jointly sell this new drug.

The deal may also have sealed Pharmacia's fate, since Pfizer has a penchant for devouring companies when the products they co-promote start selling too well. This was a major factor in Pfizer's take-over of Warner-Lambert, which gave them Lipitor, a cholesterol-lowering agent that eventually created sales of $11 billion per year.

As I listened to Fred's voicemail, his stern message startled me. He got to the point right away. Pfizer was going to buy Pharmacia. Fred said that Pfizer had made a great offer, which would result in an almost 40 percent premium over Pharmacia's current share price. There was no way Fred or the board of directors could say no to such a premium. Fred ended the call by encouraging everyone to keep working on their business.

When I hung up, my head was spinning.

Pfizer had developed a fearsome reputation for what they did to employees of the companies they bought. It could be summed up in three simple words: They fired them.

Successful Beyond Belief

When Pfizer made the decision to buy Pharmacia, they were the most successful drug company in the entire pharmaceutical business. They had grown from $3 billion in sales in 1990 to $26 billion in 2001—much faster growth than any other major drug company.[3] Their U.S. sales force was number one in productivity,[4] and the Pharmacia acquisition would vault them into the number one position in size, with $50 billion in sales.

Such results don't make anyone humble, and Pfizer employees were considered by industry-watchers to be the most arrogant in the business. Many other companies made it a practice to hate them. Some competing sales people called Pfizer sales reps "robots," or "Kool-Aid drinking drones,"[5] a reference to both Pfizer's rigorous sales training as well as the fact that many of their reps were former military officers.[6]

Pharmacia's employees had the Pfizer/Warner-Lambert merger to look to as a sign of things to come. The rumor within Pharmacia was that most of the U.S. Warner-Lambert employees had left after the take-over. But the employees at Pharmacia were not the only ones concerned about Pfizer's offer. Investors were also skeptical of this acquisition, and Pfizer's stock immediately tumbled.

Later on the day Pfizer's offer was announced, Fred Hassan continued in the open and forthright style he was known for. After fielding media calls in the morning, he scheduled a phone and video conference with his employees around the globe for the afternoon.[7]

He was serious when he appeared on the television screen and started off by telling us that from the first week since he had taken the helm at Pharmacia, he had been getting feelers from other companies about a merger, but that he had always told them to stay away. He tried to explain to us what had happened during the last three months, when talks had gotten a lot more serious between Pfizer and Pharmacia. He said that some weeks earlier he had received a very serious number, which he had taken to Pharmacia's board of directors. From there on, it was simple.

There was no way Pharmacia could deliver the kind of return that this deal would give the shareholder. Fred also noted that Pfizer's stock "should not have dropped more than 10 percent at the most today. But it dropped more than 10 percent. My feeling is that one reason the stock dropped more is that there is some concern in the financial community."

The employees who listened to his speech could see and hear that this was a difficult announcement for Fred. He would lose his job as CEO, and that was a position no money could buy. Fred's most important objective, however, was to calm Pharmacia's employees. He told us that he had been through many mergers, and, "I can tell you, in all these, that I've seen there is a lot of fear, a lot of concern. In the end, the vast majority of people come out okay. They find ways to take care of themselves and their own lives." Then he added something interesting that made everyone listen even harder, "Also, I was talking to Hank McKinnell, the Chief Executive Officer of Pfizer about his plans. He assured me that while his immediate senior management team is likely to be more heavily tilted towards Pfizer, they're going to have very open minds when it comes to the other people. Not quite the same as the Warner-Lambert situation."

He undoubtedly sensed the unease among his audience, because as he looked into the television camera, he added a personal story to try to convince everyone that we would be fine. He explained that someone from Pfizer had said, "Please tell me the names of good people; because we are looking for good people. We want to find an excuse to get rid of our mediocre people via this transaction." Referring to Pfizer he said, "Because they respect our people and they know that there are a lot of special people who joined this company, there is in fact certain openness to how we're going to integrate this company."

The Bloodbath

If Fred Hassan had been able to look into the future and read Pfizer's first quarterly report in 2004—a year and a half later—he might have chosen different words. There was no way he could have known about the bloodbath Pfizer was about to unleash at Pharmacia. In the year following the acquisition, Pfizer terminated 11,596 Pharmacia employees—more than half the U.S. employees. During the same time period only 1,452 Pfizer employees were let go.[8] And it didn't stop there, over the following two years Pfizer fired thousands more.

But while Fred Hassan might not have known the extent of the layoffs, he had a notion of what might happen to all those people he had hired away from other employers. During an employee meeting, he again repeated his concerns about how Pfizer behaved in the past. "The challenge for them is, and I have said this to Hank McKinnell: Don't treat this merger the way you did the Warner-Lambert merger because this is a different company."

My colleagues and I agreed that Fred felt sincerely regretful about the situation, although we concluded that a small part of his sadness was related to the fact that he was about to lose his own job and have to report to Pfizer's CEO. His parting words at the conference were: "I'm sad, because we were having fun together. And somehow I feel we've been stopped. Because we were on a great journey. But that's all I can say about that. You know how I feel."

We sure did.

Finally, Fred waved goodbye and said, "I'm optimistic about you. Whether you stay here or you land elsewhere, we're going to be fine because we are good people."

After the announcement, some wiped tears from their eyes and most went back to their offices and started updating their resumés and returning calls to headhunters that they had ignored prior to the big news. The mood among senior management was especially sour. They, of all people, would have no future with Pfizer.

McKinnell's Choice

At this point in time, only one man really knew what would happen to Pharmacia's employees. His name was Hank McKinnell, CEO of Pfizer, and he had a scary track record in this area. *Business Week*'s Amy Barrett wrote an article that gave an unusual glimpse into Hank's thinking, describing a meeting between Pfizer's CEO and Anthony Wild, former president of Warner-Lambert.[9] They were working on the integration of their two companies in early 2000 and had dinner in a Paris restaurant when, according to Wild, McKinnell observed that he'd become convinced that Pfizer managers might be the best choice for key positions in the combined company. Wild claimed that his Warner-Lambert executives in attendance were stunned, and took the comment as an indication that they had no future with Pfizer. "I saw a few jaws dropping," Wild stated. According to *Business Week*, after the acquisition most of the Warner-Lambert managers left or were let go.

In spite of his penchant for firing people, in a letter to all Pharmacia employees, dated August 12, 2002, Dr. McKinnell claimed that Pfizer was truly committed to doing what they could to create new opportunities, for example by limiting external hiring to only those jobs they needed to fill right away. When the acquisition was completed, McKinnell stated, Pfizer would be a fast-growing organization, with many career opportunities.[10]

When I read this letter, I suspected it painted a brighter future than the one we would come to know. We all knew what he had done when he took over Warner-Lambert; clearly most mergers result in job losses. My concern was that while it is illegal to discriminate based on race or age, it is not illegal to discriminate based on which company an employee works for. And Pfizer is a company famous for such discrimination, which I think is a sign of an insecure management, in fear of losing power. Just like nepotism should be kept at bay in any well managed enterprise, so should any discrimination.

When I returned to my home in New Jersey and talked to my wife about the situation, we rapidly agreed we preferred the security and stability of my staying with the company, if possible. We had moved about eight times over the last ten years. The last thing we wanted to do was to move again. Then again, we realized, the whole issue could be moot. It would probably be months before we even knew whether I would have a job. We had two small boys, one of them only a year old, the other six. Things could get dicey if my job disappeared, so I knew I had to work hard on impressing the people from Pfizer.

TWO

The Conquerors

PHARMACIA'S EXQUISITE OFFICES WERE nestled in the rolling hills of central New Jersey. If a person didn't know that this was the corporate headquarters of a pharmaceutical company, they might have mistaken it for a well-maintained college campus, with low-slung brick buildings topped by towers and turrets and a cobblestone square complete with a clock steeple. Inside, the individual offices were spacious, interior glass walls letting the sunshine pass through. The furniture was made of light birch in true Nordic style. In short, these were the most pleasant corporate headquarter offices I had seen anywhere. I liked it.

I also genuinely liked my coworkers. Pharmacia didn't feel like a stuffy old corporation, like many of its competitors. People were happy and energetic, frequently arriving as early as seven and often not leaving until the same time in the evening.

In exchange for their efforts, these people were well taken care of. The company had a small store with dry cleaning pick-up, postal services, and a spacious cafeteria serving everything from gourmet sandwiches to a fresh salad bar, ice cream, pizzas, and high-quality Mexican, Italian, and American cuisine. They even had a fashionable gym on the premises, where employees enervated by long meetings could work out and refresh. In December, employees could choose from a range of corporate gifts, from DVD players to small television sets.

Preparation for Take-Over

The positive atmosphere vanished quickly in the wake of the news of the take-over. I also noticed the change in my workload. The request for business updates and presentations to Pharmacia's management dwindled rapidly. But the initial slack was soon taken up by requests from Pfizer to teach *them* about our business. Most people in middle management grasped this opportunity with gusto. They still had the opportunity to show Pfizer how indispensable they were.

As time went by, Pfizer's management spent more and more time directly with their Pharmacia counterparts and elaborate presentations soon became the staple of most workdays. When fall of 2002 approached in New Jersey and the leaves turned and started to cover the cobblestones, Pharmacia's employees were busy toiling over PowerPoint presentations. They worked hard and willingly shared as much information as they could, hoping this would reassure and appease their future masters. I participated as much as anyone in this exercise, though I couldn't help but think of cattle on their way through a slaughter chute.

The Uncomfortable Question

On one memorable occasion, Pfizer's entire senior team visited Pharmacia. Security was very tight—for the first time we had to show our employee ID cards when we entered the lunch room where the meeting was held. First up to talk was Hank McKinnell. He told us that a large part of his senior team would be eligible for retirement within five years. That was a good thing for us, he said, and then he quipped, "And for me."

At another meeting, Fred Hassan, our CEO, opened up the floor to questions that hadn't been prescreened. I couldn't resist writing on my little white question card, "If you hadn't agreed to a friendly acquisition, would this have been a hostile takeover?" As the question was read, Fred's face froze, then darkened. "No comment," he said abruptly, and pouted with his lower lip.

A third meeting took place when one of Pfizer's HR people, dressed in a red leather skirt, visited Pharmacia. Apparently, she had worked as a lawyer in a prior life, and she came off as fairly arrogant to the assembled Pharmacia crowd. When pressed with more and more pointed questions, she yelled to the packed room, "You should realize that it is *Pfizer* taking over *you* and *not* the other way around." The wolf had just dropped her sheep's clothing.

An Early Offer

In December 2002, the first Pharmacia employees started getting job offers from Pfizer. One of them was Isadora Pelozzi, who reported to me. It wasn't surprising that she would be one of the first to get an offer; she was smart and had a perfect career record. But there may have been another reason that Pfizer looked to her leadership so early on in the process: Isadora was the key person in charge of a new product launch within my group, a product that would revolutionize therapy for patients with an affliction called acromegaly. These patients would become giants and die early unless they were given appropriate therapy. As a matter of fact, we had hired Richard Kiel, the actor who played "Jaws" in two James Bond movies, to be our spokesperson, since he suffered from this particular disease.

Isadora was, understandably, excited when she first heard that Pfizer was interested in her. But she became concerned when she got her offer letter. Among other things, they had capped her bonus at a lower level than Pharmacia's upper limit.[1] To Isadora this welcome felt like a cold embrace. She knew she was good; she knew that her project knowledge made her one of the most important staff members in my group. Pfizer really needed her, so why would they treat her this way?

What she might not have realized was that Pfizer was a company where senior employees often had toiled for ten, twenty, or thirty years with minimal raises. According to some recruiters, this had resulted in a pay that was 20 percent lower than what Pharmacia offered. Such a situation is not uncommon and even has a name: Salary compression.

But Isadora hadn't succeeded by sitting back and letting her salary be compressed. She did what any good businessperson would do; she e-mailed her prospective new boss at Pfizer and asked a few polite questions. Her new boss, Harry Otter, had just been promoted from director to vice president in anticipation of the acquisition. As a matter of fact, a whole slew of promotions were announced at Pfizer in anticipation of the merger—they were positioned to be the new lords of the conquered Pharmacia masses.

Never Ask Questions

Like a good soldier, Isadora started her e-mail by saying that she was very excited about the opportunity to join Pfizer, but added, "You are asking me to come in and run what will be a billion-dollar endocrine business. I hope that you understand my need to ensure that I run my personal business effectively also."[2] She pointed out that she was surprised that her bonus might be reduced in future years and wanted to know what her title would be. She also wanted to know how many people she would have in her new group, and whether Pfizer would honor her current five weeks of vacation.

In response, Isadora got a voicemail from Mr. Otter saying that he had forwarded most of her questions to Pfizer's human resources department. A couple of days later, Isadora had a long talk with Harry Otter on the phone. They discussed the head-count needed to run the business, and he described Pfizer's business model as being in flux. Isadora asked if there were any information he could send to help her "understand the fluxing."

Aside from several more voicemails that Isadora left over the following days with Otter, they didn't speak until Monday, January 13, 2003. He was brief and very clear: Pfizer was *retracting* their job offer, primarily because he felt that Isadora wasn't a good fit for Pfizer. Isadora's jaw dropped, and for a few seconds time stood still. She wasn't quite sure she had heard him right. Isadora was good, smart, and decisive. She knew that not only was she one of the best marketing people Pharmacia had ever hired, Pfizer really *needed* her if they wanted continuity in the launch preparations for this important new drug. And now, she was being canned because she asked questions?

Isadora's Response

She stayed cool and professional. In her mind, Pfizer had finally shown its true face, but she knew she mustn't overreact. So she waited a couple of days before writing back to Harry Otter. She spoke her mind, and to make sure everyone got the message, she copied a number of people.

Isadora didn't hold back any punches. After having calmly recapped the events leading up to the retraction of her job offer, she couldn't contain herself anymore and wrote, "As I said, I respect decisions, even bad ones. At least they allow people to move forward. *But my God, could you not have come to this determination earlier? How did this offer and retraction fiasco happen?* You only want people who will jump blindly to you?"[3]

Isadora also realized that this incident would have reverberations far beyond herself and ended her missive by telling Pfizer that her people were still with the company and that they now had much higher anxiety levels than what might be necessary.

Isadora's comments would turn out to be much more prescient than she could ever have imagined. The news of her fate swept through Pharmacia like a prairie fire. Everyone was talking about the fact that if you ask questions when you get an offer from Pfizer, they will retract it. This episode confirmed that Pfizer was a company with a very different attitude toward employees than Pharmacia. It certainly reminded us of Fred's words—and our fear—about "the other horror stories about what happened to Warner-Lambert."

It is worth noting that Pfizer later went on to launch the drug Isadora was going to put on the market without the help from anyone on her marketing team. The launch turned out to be a complete and utter disaster, with the drug not selling half of Pfizer's forecasts.[4]

Selling Out

Meanwhile, according to a revised employment contract for top Pharmacia officers, filed December 20, 2002, with the SEC,[5] Fred and his direct reports had agreed to an unsavory pact with Pfizer, promising not to hire any employees from Pharmacia in return for three years' base salary and bonus. This meant that if our top management, including Fred, started work at another company, they wouldn't be able to bring aboard any of their old colleagues or subordinates until such a person had left Pfizer, or until two years had passed.

As the actual takeover approached, the messages from Pharmacia's HR department also took on a new tone. In an e-mail sent in March of 2003, Pharmacia's managers were told that they were forbidden to give references to employees who were leaving the company, "The company does not provide written or oral references for current of former employees. Pharmacia has adopted this policy to ensure all employees receive consistent treatment."[6]

The e-mail caused an outcry at Pharmacia, since abiding by this edict would make it all but impossible for anyone to get a new job. Despite one's abilities and job history, without excellent references from prior supervisors one stands no chance of getting a job offer.

I was furious when I read this, and so were many of my colleagues. I found it reprehensible that the people in charge of the company first negotiated golden severance packages for themselves and then stuck it to the rank and file employees. So I decided to write a response to Adrian Hoffman, Pharmacia's Senior Vice President of Human Resources. I told him that enforcement of this policy could result in employees being locked out of the job market. And I ended my e-mail suggesting, "You can retract the policy on references. Or you can issue an additional policy, saying that

Pharmacia and Pfizer forbid the use of any personal references when hiring new employees."[7]

After clicking on the "send" button, I printed out a copy of my letter and took it to my boss, Darren McAllister. He read it in silence, then looked up at me. He only had one question, "Did you already send this, Peter?" He wasn't smiling.

In the end, my letter had no impact on the "no reference" policy.

THREE

The Art of Firing People

As the April 2003 Pfizer take-over date rapidly approached, some more Pharmacia employees received job offers from the new organization, many of whom said no thanks—but many didn't hear anything at all from Pfizer. At the same time we silently watched as wave after wave of Pfizer managers were promoted into new positions and the level of cynicism at Pharmacia grew day by day.

As the merger loomed, those of us with managerial responsibilities were told that we needed to learn how to properly fire our subordinates. That was when the consultants specializing in "career transition" moved in. By now, we really felt like cattle on our way to the slaughter chute, certain that after we had killed off our subordinates, we'd be next.

To learn the art of firing people we were asked to participate in a large meeting at an off-site conference center. From the outside this looked like any regular business meeting. People had to sign in and everyone got a nametag, lest unauthorized employees or—worst of all—a journalist try to get the inside scoop. A man and a woman from the out-sourcing firm started by telling us how their service made them a productive part of the food-chain. Firing employees had been elevated to an art form, apparently. Despite my mixed feelings, I couldn't help being fascinated by their presentation. It was like listening to a law enforcement officer explaining how to most effectively immobilize a prisoner.

No Crying

We were told that we needed to choose an appropriate setting for the termination meetings. If we expected trouble, we could have an "exit team" waiting around the corner, invisible to the unsuspecting target. The exit team could, if needed, carry out a screaming and panicked employee that refused to leave, I suppose.

After having welcomed the employee we were going to terminate, we were told to "express interest in the person's comfort in the room." I guess the firing manager was supposed to ask if it was too warm, too cold, or just right. Or perhaps make sure that the victim found their chair comfortable.

It was important to note that "small talk" should be kept brief, e.g. two minutes. The presenters—by now I was thinking of them as "Terminators"—strongly suggested not waiting too long before letting the ax fall.

The second step was to "set the stage." Here the manager should express his understanding of the acquisition. To be honest, I didn't see how saying, "Pharmacia shareholders will make a lot of money on this transaction, but many of us will be out of a job, so let's be happy for our shareholders," would go over too well.

The third step was to actually do the deed. For any trigger-happy supervisor who didn't get to play dictator at home, this was the moment when he took control of another human being's life. He should announce the "separation," another euphemism for "firing," perhaps intended to make people associate it with simply being apart, like a vacation—a long vacation.

I could see necks crane as we got to this point in the meeting. There were hundreds of managers in the room and you could hear a pin drop. We all waited for the next set of instructions. The man at the podium explained that it was "imperative to plan and rehearse the statement that announces the separation." We should also present the decision as definite and final, and we might want to repeat what we had just said to our victim.

Once that was done, we should present the reasons for termination in such a way that the separated employee clearly understood and remembered that he was being fired. That would be for the really hard-headed ones who didn't listen, I guess. Every organization has a few of those. My mind started to wander and I thought of the day when I would have to fire Isadora Pelozzi. Perhaps I would say, "You're being separated because you asked questions. We don't ask questions at Pfizer."

I heard the male Terminator at the podium say something about how important it was to show compassion. Crying together with the targeted employee, however, was *not* recommended.

After having gone through some mandatory catch-phrases, such as "You should know that a generous separation kit has been created for all former Pharmacia employees losing their jobs due to the acquisition," we were shown the final step. The final step was to "listen and allow time to react and ask questions." It was important to allow eye contact and to show that we were listening. If we didn't feel compassionate, clearly we were supposed to pretend that we were.

In short, the day was a miniature course in emotional manipulation, with the objective of getting rid of people without causing a scene.

We were also instructed that company policy was not to provide any references, as if anyone could have forgotten the infamous memo on this topic. So, "Off you go, you've done a great job, but we're *not* going to tell anyone, because that could be unfair to others."

At that point, I thought the meeting was over, but it wasn't. Next we were going to learn how to handle the "difficult employees"—the ones who won't walk docilely through the slaughter chute.

The Very Angry Person

First we had to learn to deal with "The Very Angry Person,"[1] and I half-expected that they would bring in uniformed security personnel and show pictures of Taser guns on the big screen in front of us. Instead we got another lecture in psychology.

We were told that we should "acknowledge the employee's feelings," but that we could not "respond in kind." I guess that meant we shouldn't yell back at the distraught mother who now had no way of supporting her three children. We were told that the best response to the angry employee was to repeat the statements, describing the support the company would offer.

We were also warned that we couldn't expect to turn angry employees into docile ones, since "only proper counseling can do that." I couldn't help but wonder how counseling was going to feed those three kids. We were also supposed to be firm, saying, "I'm afraid we're past the point of looking at alternatives. The decision is made and it's final." If the situation got completely out of control, we were asked to leave the room and let HR or a consultant from the company that specialized in firing employees take over. We were also told to notify security in advance if we expected a "difficult situation."

The Emotional Employee

Then we had "The Emotional Employee."[2] The best advice was apparently to remain calm and in control and to acknowledge the employee's feelings. But crying together with the fired employee was still not part of the response. If the employee went on crying for too long, a few minutes break was suggested.

They also gave us some great statements to use, such as, "I know this is a difficult situation, but I do believe you'll do better than you think." Obviously the Terminators who did the talking had no idea if anyone would do better than they thought, demonstrating again how manipulative the entire process was.

The Out-of-Control Reaction

We were told about the worst potential reaction: "The Out-of-Control Reaction."[3] That reaction might indicate deeper problems and the need for professional help. They didn't say we should call in men in white coats, but I have to admit that my imagination had begun to really run wild by this point in the session. I was disappointed when we were simply advised to remain firm and unwavering.

Finally, we were given a "script" to use when firing an employee. It ended, "I know this is difficult news to hear. If I can be of assistance to you in any way, please come to me." Too bad they had just forbidden us to do the one thing that could really have assisted a terminated employee—give them a reference.

FOUR

Crimes and Misdemeanors

FROM THE BEGINNING OF MY TIME AT PHARMACIA, the flagship drug of my endocrinology franchise had been Genotropin, a human growth hormone. Though we sold it for use in both short children and adults with growth hormone deficiency, the big market was children—they had to inject the drug daily for many years until they reached their adult height. A patient base like that made for stable sales that didn't fluctuate a lot. Our only worries were our three major competitors, each with their own genetically engineered growth hormone, virtually identical to ours.

This situation resulted in an unusual practice called "rotation," in which doctors played "eeny meeny miney mo," giving the first patient our drug, the second patient a competitor's drug, and so on. They did this so that they could enjoy the meetings, travel, and other incentive programs that all pharmaceutical companies provided. "Why go to an exotic resort only once a year when you can go four times?" appeared to be the general motto among physicians. This was one of my first concerns as I started my new job back in the summer of 2001. I found out that we paid for many hundreds of physicians to go to wonderful locations in the Caribbean and Mexico. Against AMA guidelines we paid their way, and we even allowed spouses to attend for a very low price. The way this was explained to me was that Pharmacia didn't consider them to be regular doctors. They were "investigators." Needless to say, few of them did any real studies. To become an investigator was all too simple: fill out a form with information about how much Genotropin they had given a particular patient, write down a few patient measurements, send it to Pharmacia and—voila—you're an "investigator." I asked Darren McAllister about this in the fall of 2001, and he told me that Pharmacia's legal department had approved the program.

An Unusual Memo

Darren McAllister apparently had his own concerns about my area of responsibility, and one of the first documents he gave me was a memo he had written to all the foreign affiliates and to our U.S. sales department, with a copy to Pharmacia's senior management. It was titled "Growth Hormone in Aging Patients."[1]

The memo went on to explain that there had been much media attention about the use of growth hormone in elderly patients to reduce the impact of aging. The memo stated in bold letters that "Pharmacia does not, may not and will not promote or encourage the usage of our products outside of the approved labeling."

Anyone who works in pharmaceutical marketing knows that it is illegal to promote a product beyond the FDA-approved labeling. A company can't say the drug works for a disease or use which has not been approved by the FDA. Companies that have been caught doing so have paid hundreds of millions of dollars in fines. The question in my mind was simple: Since everyone knew this basic fact of pharmaceutical sales and marketing, why the memo?

I knew that Darren was the epitome of integrity, so I didn't believe for a second that he would do anything wrong, but he had taken responsibility for my area only recently. Who knew what had been the practice before he came on? Or what people might *still* have been doing? I would get many opportunities during the coming years to reflect on these initial concerns.

More Discoveries

My worries increased as my first months with Pharmacia passed. I discovered more and more details about our business that concerned me. I researched the situation and learned that giving a rebate to doctors who did off-label prescriptions could be regarded as an improper incentive, which could be a violation of anti-kickback statutes.[2] I also learned that we could be even worse off if we provided free drugs. Cold chills started to creep down my spine. We were giving all kinds of rebates to all kinds of centers, including doctors that specialized in anti-aging. We were also giving away free drugs to virtually *all* new patients for the first few months, before they got approval for insurance coverage. (This was a very expensive drug costing $20,000 per year—not something patients simply picked up in a pharmacy.)

My primary concern, however, was not sales we shouldn't have made, but how to increase overall sales. After all, that was my job—to be a healthcare hitman. Exploring my options led to the next anomaly: 90 percent of our sales went to pediatric patients, and only 10 percent to adult patients. But our sales efforts didn't reflect this ratio: Half our sales force focused on the adult area, and seventeen of the top twenty bonus payouts went to sales reps targeting the adult area.[3]

This made no sense from a business point of view. Why give bonuses mainly to the sales people that generated just 10 percent of the business? Why push sales to the adult market? Did its potential really justify the expense?

The reason most sales went to children was that they needed very high doses, costing a lot of money, for many years. Adults, on the other hand, used very low doses and often stopped treatment after only a few months. Based on the doctors who wrote adult prescriptions, dosing and length of treatment, we concluded that most of the adult sales were being prescribed for off-label anti-aging treatments.

Bonus Formulas That Didn't Make Sense

I got even more concerned when I saw how we calculated bonuses. We rewarded sales representatives per new patient, not per sales dollar. In this way, a rep who called on a doctor who brought in hundreds of low-paying adult patients could make much more money than a rep who sold to a doctor with a few high-paying pediatric patients.

Suspicious, I tried to compare how profitable these two areas were. Apparently no one had ever done such an exercise, and I had a hard time extracting this information from my U.S. marketing team. When we finalized the analysis, I was in for a shocker: We made *no* money on the adult franchise. We also projected that we wouldn't make any money over the next five years. It was time for some major change in how we ran our business, and it was time to tell the Pharmacia lawyers what I had learned. [4]

Criminal Liability

But the surprises didn't stop there. One day a Pharmacia lawyer left a document I had never seen before on my desk. As I read the words, the hair on the back of my neck stood straight up.

> *The 21st paragraph of the United States Code 333(f) states that: ". . . whoever knowingly distributes, or possesses with intent to distribute, human growth hormone for any use in humans other than the treatment of a disease or other recognized medical condition, where such use has been authorized by the Secretary of Health and Human Services under 21 U.S.C. 355 and pursuant to the order of a physician, is guilty of an offense punishable by not more than 5 years in prison."*

Anyone who works in marketing knows that off-label marketing is illegal and can result in fines for the company, but I had never before heard of any drug where illegal distribution could result in jail. I looked at my business card. It said "Peter Rost, M.D., Vice President, Endocrine Care, Healthcare Hitman." Actually, it didn't say the last two words, but it could have. To be a vice president, I thought, would be enough to put me in a bad position if the Feds came looking at our business. I had to take action.

The Internal Investigation

I spent the following months working closely with Pharmacia's legal department and many of the employees in the U.S. group were interviewed. By the time we were done, we had new people in the U.S. marketing department and had created a new sales incentive system that didn't reward off-label sales. We also stopped giving all those rebates to the anti-aging centers and all kinds of other rebates to various wholesalers and pharmacy benefit managers. The effect didn't take long to appear—Genotropin sales went through the roof.

As a direct result of these changes, in 2003 Genotropin became the best performing product vs. budget, if products with sales of more than $100 million were compared. We increased sales by 46 percent and came in more than 30 percent over forecast.[5] This was the best performance in the history of Genotropin.

But I still had concerns. Pharmacia's legal department had helped us stop many questionable practices, but they hadn't stopped all of them. Now we had new bosses from Pfizer, so we set out to inform them about what had been going on and perhaps get them to agree to take additional action.

Breaking the News to Pfizer

On a beautiful day in October 2002,[6] a small group from my department went to Pfizer's headquarters in Manhattan to discuss our programs and concerns. (None of us had yet been offered jobs with Pfizer.)

Pfizer's offices were shoddy in comparison to Pharmacia's headquarters. The corridors were small and cramped, and the carpet looked like it hadn't been replaced in thirty years. Even Pfizer's vice presidents were squeezed into offices so small they could stand and touch virtually everything in their room. It didn't look like a fun environment to work in; it reminded us of a beehive.

They put us in a dinky conference room, and when the last one of us had arrived, the Pfizer people joined. Their employees appeared different too: Tense, harried, and stressed. Many were quite old in relation to the positions they held—promotions were few and far between. Compared to Pharmacia, this was a different country.

I had a lot on my mind, not all of which I got a chance to discuss. After some of my U.S. marketing people had departed six months earlier, I went through their files, which were treasure troves of illegal marketing. I found contracts that paid $50,000 to individual anti-aging physicians for "consulting" services; I discovered an outfit in Canada that was going to help establish business for these physicians, to which we paid a $10,000 monthly retainer. Sales people came forward telling us how they had been forced to do off-label promotion. One sales person in Chicago had been terminated because he had refused. In the years past, Pharmacia had conducted an annual ethics certification of our sales reps and many had stated that they had been forced to do off-label promotion. It was bad, really bad, and I wasn't sure if Pharmacia's legal department had done everything it could.

Pens on Fire

What really scared Pfizer were the business practices still in place at Pharmacia, the ones I had warned Pharmacia's legal department about, but that they hadn't stopped. We divulged the "investigator" meetings and Caribbean trips and we described the program that supplied everyone with free drugs for several months, which could easily be seen as an inducement to off-label sales. We called this the Bridge program, since it bridged the time period until the patient got reimbursement from his insurance company with free drugs, and though fundamentally this was a well-meaning program, it could be abused. All of us had a strong incentive to explain what we had done to stop inappropriate practices, since we didn't want to be associated with any of this.

We could see the Pfizer people writing as if their pens were on fire, and they immediately requested a second meeting to review the Bridge program in detail. They were visibly shaken, and after the meeting they sent a flurry of e-mail requests for more information. We actually felt pretty good about all this—we had put the cards on the table, and we hoped our forthrightness, and the fact that we had addressed many of the problems, would help us land new jobs within Pfizer.

A Promise

I didn't just have legal issues on my mind during this time period; most of all I was concerned about my own future. After having done a number of presentations to Pfizer, I thought it was a good time to ask them what my situation with the company would be. The response came back very quickly from Pfizer's new Senior Vice President for Global Marketing. "There is no issue whatsoever on our side with your being considered for several positions,"[7] Wyler Jennings wrote.

I was relieved. I knew there weren't too many vice president positions out there in a shrinking industry, especially with all the Pharmacia employees now looking for jobs. I was also confident that Pharmacia's management would give me a strong endorsement for a new job with Pfizer. In fact, Gertrude Hawk, Pharmacia's president, had written an e-mail to me saying, "You have made outstanding contributions to our organization that surpass by far the length of your tenure, and I sincerely hope you'll have a long career with the new company. If I can be of any assistance to you, now or in the future, please don't hesitate to call me."[8]

While I didn't have a specific job offer in my hand yet, things were moving in the right direction, and I started to feel comfortable. It was also a relief to have reviewed some of the legal concerns we had with Pfizer; hopefully, this would make them understand how responsibly we had managed the situation and how we could assist them in resolving some of the remaining issues.

Pharmacia's CEO Receives a Warning

Later in 2003, I got another piece of alarming news. One of the most famous professors in the endocrinology area told me that a group of renowned endocrinologists around the world had been very worried a couple of years earlier about the direction the Genotropin franchise was taking in the U.S. The fact that Pharmacia paid for and included many off-label patients in their database was of particular concern to them.

They had been so worried, in fact, that they had written a letter directly to Fred Hassan—Pharmacia's CEO. I asked if I could see the letter. Lo and behold, back on August 21, 2000, one year before I started my new job at Pharmacia, he and many others had indeed spelled out their concerns to Fred.[9]

Dear Fred Hassan,

> *Since you had personally devoted much interest into the KIGS/KIMS* [Pharmacia International Growth/Metabolic Database] *process we take the liberty to address you directly without considering in-house aspects of hierarchy.*

> *We—the members of the Strategic Planning Committee of KIGS and KIMS—would like to express our most sincere concerns about pending decisions by the management of Pharmacia which will have major adverse implications for these databases.*

> *One relates to the intention to incorporate patient groups other than those with GHD or short stature into the existing databases.*

KIGS and KIMS were two outcomes databases that tracked patients. GHD was an abbreviation for "growth hormone deficiency," a condition for which the FDA had approved Genotropin. A competing drug was approved for short stature a year after this letter. So when this professor asked Fred not to include patients with other indications, he was referring to all the indications for which Genotropin *was not approved.* The professor also wrote in an e-mail to me, "I told them that it was first when you joined that my confidence in Pharmacia returned. I told them about your predecessor's off-label marketing."[10]

What I didn't discover until later when I started to connect many loose documents, was that on January 14, 2000, Fred had received a letter from a prominent anti-aging physician. The letter was written on the "The Renaissance Longevity Center" stationary and invited Hassan to a "strategic alliance" for the "most aggressive ethical campaign ever launched for the marketing of growth hormone injections."

Fred sent the letter with an annotation in his own handwriting "Please follow-up/ack, etc., FH," to his direct reports and it ended up on the desk of the person responsible for Genotropin at that time. On February 3, 2000, the same anti-aging physician wrote a two-page letter to the Vice President of Endocrine Care, summarizing a telephone conference they had on January 28, 2000. Among other things he wanted to discuss were the ability for the longevity centers to purchase growth hormone at quantity discount prices and other benefits that Pharmacia could provide them. On May 1, 2000, the US marketing director for Genotropin signed a "$50,000" consulting agreement with the anti-aging physicians and the rest is history; sales of Genotropin for anti-aging purposes took off.

FIVE

You're Fired!

SHORTLY AFTER WE HAD FINISHED ANOTHER ROUND of presentations to Pfizer, 2003 arrived and, with it, a surprise for Pharmacia and Pfizer management. It came in the form of a headline in the *New York Times*: "Whistle-Blower Accuses Wyeth of Tax Dodges."[1] Their surprise was that I was the whistleblower.

Before I joined Pharmacia in 2001, I'd been employed by Wyeth, where I was managing director for the Nordic region in Europe, with four country managers reporting to me. Sadly, I'd been asked to leave that position after only two years, in spite of delivering one of the best performances in the entire company.

David Cay Johnston and Melody Petersen from the *New York Times* described what happened: "A former international executive for Wyeth, the big drug company, uncovered a worldwide practice of cheating foreign governments out of taxes, only to be demoted after notifying senior executives, according to documents in a state lawsuit he filed against the company." Since I don't want to comment directly on this situation, I'll simply tell you what the *New York Times* wrote. According to the article, the chief financial officer of the Swedish subsidiary confided to me during his exit interview that he had "been lying to our auditors, Arthur Andersen, about payouts to Swedish executives that were arranged to escape taxes." I immediately contacted the company's outside lawyers, auditors, and company management. Two months later, the *New York Times* wrote, Wyeth's primary auditors—Arthur Andersen—instructed

Wyeth that corrected tax returns had to be filed immediately and that even with such action "the risk for indictment for tax fraud is not set aside."

The article also stated that John R. Stafford, Wyeth's chairman, approved a plan to reimburse the Swedish executives for taxes that they owed, "according to an internal document he signed that was filed with the lawsuit." The *Times* finally described how I was summoned to London, where I was told I was being transferred to the United States. There, I was given a windowless office in suburban Philadelphia "with a staff of eight, compared with the 175 people he oversaw in Sweden."

The next day, Paul Beckett and Jathon Sapsford wrote an article titled, "Wyeth Ex-Officer's Suit Revisits Foreign Tax Issues"[2] in the *Wall Street Journal*. They wrote that "allegations that some overseas colleagues at the pharmaceutical company avoided paying taxes highlights a problem that was prevalent among U.S. companies decades ago, but one that experts thought had changed." The *Wall Street Journal* reported that during the past decade, Wyeth had made changes in their reporting policies in some countries, sometimes after Wyeth had been contacted by local tax authorities. In the United Kingdom, for instance, tax authorities had, ten years earlier, requested the names of Wyeth U.K. employees, and the amount of bonuses they received. A spokesperson for Wyeth said the company had provided that information annually since then. In France, a Wyeth official said, "From the mid-1990s, we have filed all proper returns and paid proper taxes through our French subsidiary." The official, however, declined to comment on the company's tax reporting prior to that time.

It was an interesting article and I hoped that people who read it would understand why I had been forced to take action.

The Initial Reaction

I should point out that these two articles, and many others, hadn't simply happened by themselves. I had worked with newspapers on two continents for months to set off a full media campaign aimed at publicizing the information in my lawsuit against Wyeth. This was part of my strategy to prove my case before the eyes of all my colleagues who had wondered why I had left my managing director assignment so suddenly. It was also part of my strategy to put pressure on Wyeth.

This approach involved a calculated but significant risk—I couldn't predict how Pharmacia and Pfizer would react. When I read the *New York Times* article, my heart was racing. I had no idea what would happen. It felt strange going to the office that morning, realizing that suddenly everyone would look at me differently.

Initially, what I had feared most about suing Wyeth was the negative impact it could have on my career. But I had concluded that this was the only way to win against Wyeth, and, once I started thinking in those terms, I focused on that short-term objective. I also gambled that Pfizer wouldn't be foolish enough to try to immediately dismiss an employee surrounded by a team of lawyers.

I realized that the article would set off warning bells around Pharmacia, so I immediately contacted Fred Hassan and his direct reports. This wasn't easy or pleasant, but I had started a dangerous process and I needed to do what I could to ensure things didn't spin out of control. First I met with Gunnar Anderson, the man in charge of research at Pharmacia. He said he had already seen the news clippings and would discuss the situation with Fred. Later that day I met Veronica Castalia, who was in charge of Corporate Affairs. Veronica was very polite. She listened intently but was very, very careful not to say anything. I could tell that my visit probably hadn't helped to further my cause. Later I talked with a good friend of mine (and fellow Swede) in her department. She suggested to Castalia that Pharmacia "give the guy some help" but had been told "that's not how we do things in the U.S."

Gertrude Hawk, Pharmacia's president, initially agreed to see me and seemed to be quite receptive, but then her secretary cancelled and made it clear that I shouldn't make another appointment.

Fred Hassan remained my biggest worry. I knew anything associated with Wyeth could be sensitive to him because of his relationship with that company. He and Bob Essner—the CEO of Wyeth—were very close. Bob had reported to Fred for a long time when they were both at Wyeth, before Fred left to take over Pharmacia. Bob stayed behind and was later promoted to CEO of Wyeth, and the two men remained close friends. I knew of their friendship because when I had been hired almost two years earlier, Fred had interviewed me and his major concern was what Bob would say if I left Wyeth. This confirmed to me just how close-knit the pharmaceutical industry is.

During my job interview Fred told me that when he had hired Gertrude Hawk from Wyeth, people at Wyeth had not been happy. He repeatedly asked what the reaction would be if I left. He was especially interested in knowing whether it had been Bob Essner or someone else who had brought me back to the U.S. from managing the Nordic region. I told him that I didn't think it was Bob, and he had seemed satisfied with that.

No Job

The tension was about to increase. On my way home that afternoon, my attorney called and told me that he had been contacted by the Securities and Exchange Commission.[3] They asked me to come to Washington for an inquiry into the Wyeth matter. I was overjoyed; if the government got involved, I had a much better chance of prevailing in my fight against Wyeth. I had never testified before any government body; however, I felt more than ready. The one thing that I couldn't figure out was how they had been able to get the name of my attorney. Later I realized that David Cay Johnston at the *New York Times* had told me he had good contacts inside many government agencies and must have called them.

I had more serious news awaiting me when I arrived home. That same evening at about seven thirty—which happened to be Friday night—I got an e-mail from Wyler Jennings, the senior vice president at Pfizer who previously told me they were considering me for several positions. Now he took a very different tone. He wrote, "My understanding is that the only type of position you are interested in considering is at a VP level. There are a very limited number of such positions, and considering this level only, there will not be a fit with the Marketing Organization."[4]

I was surprised because I hadn't said a single word about only wanting a particular position, especially a vice president job. We simply hadn't discussed levels I was interested in. I also felt that it was rather unsophisticated to send this message on the same day the *New York Times* article appeared. It was glaringly obvious that Pfizer was suddenly in a big rush to communicate this to me, almost as if they tried to turn back the clock. The most serious problem for Pfizer was that I had also spent all that time informing them of unethical and illegal business practices within Pharmacia. It is illegal to fire someone because they have disclosed illegal or unethical activity.

Fighting Back

I spent the weekend thinking about what to do. I realized that I hadn't actually been *terminated*; there was just one particular position that had been taken away from me. I decided to make sure that Wyler Jennings understood what was at stake. I figured that perhaps they hadn't taken my legal concerns seriously and I might be able to explain why they needed me. I tooled for a long time at home on my computer to get the message just right. This is what I wrote:[5]

> Thank you for your efforts on my behalf. I really appreciate this. You know, I would have loved to work for you and I think I could have become a strong and loyal supporter of your team.
>
> Before making your final decision you also have another issue you may want to consider. The Endocrine Care department has a far greater legal liability than we have been able to talk to you about. If you lose key company

memory and competence, you will have a greater difficulty protecting your legal interests and demonstrating to the courts that you took appropriate action if charges would be filed against you. You would repeat exactly the same mistakes you did with Lipitor and Neurontin. The Endocrine Care franchise has a legal exposure to the following:

a. Distribution of a misbranded drug into interstate commerce (21 U.S.C., Sec 331, 333, 352).
b. Violation of FDCA to distribute human growth hormone for off-label use.
c. Fraud and Abuse issues including Anti-kickback statute and False Claims.

Pharmacia has for more than five years been actively promoting Genotropin for off-label usage, mainly for anti-aging purposes. For growth hormone this is a felony. Genentech settled a similar case for their human growth hormone related to same issues during 1985-1994 for $50 million. Pharmacia sales reps who did not agree to off-label promotion were fired or other adverse action was taken against them. We also have compliance records from sales reps indicating in writing that they had been forced to do off-label promotion. Pharmacia also actively encouraged off-label prescriptions through favorable contracts with distributors and doctors exclusively working in the anti-aging area. Pharmacia also paid kickbacks, sometimes in the form of "consulting agreements" of up to $50,000. Finally, Pharmacia used a vendor to help train anti-aging doctors in how to set up practice and promote anti-aging.

The Link to Fred Hassan

Meanwhile, Fred Hassan's name and his connection to Wyeth were soon pulled into the news reporting. In the ensuing media storm about the revelations in my Wyeth lawsuit, a Swedish magazine penned the headline, "Pharmacia CEO in U.S. Scandal." They especially noted that I worked at Pharmacia, that Fred Hassan was Pharmacia's CEO, and that Fred used to be a high-level executive at Wyeth until he left in 1997. I was, of course, well aware of all those facts and I was only surprised that the U.S media didn't make more of this.

The journalist ended the article, "It is not a far-fetched guess that this drive by the authorities and media will also catch the scent of Pharmacia CEO Fred Hassan, who is just waiting for the cartel supervisors in Brussels and Washington to approve Pfizer's takeover of Pharmacia."[6]

The irony of the situation was that I received this article from Pharmacia's public relations department. They had translated it for Fred and kindly sent a copy to me. Now I felt really uneasy.

Unexpected Support

In the middle of the storm surrounding the articles, a few colleagues came out supporting me. The first appeared to be my boss—Darren McAllister. He had been away on a business trip and as soon as he came back, he went by my office holding up both thumbs. That felt pretty good. Another person who came out swinging was a professor; one of our most important opinion leaders. (Pharmaceutical companies call doctors at the forefront of science who present to other doctors "opinion leaders.") This professor wrote a letter to Fred Hassan, saying, "I am a bit concerned about the Pfizer takeover and the effect that could have on endocrine care. In my view you have put together an excellent team of people for endocrine care. I don't think it would be good for the business if this team is broken up. I am very pleased with the way Peter Rost is handling the business. He has a very good reputation among the endocrine community. The recent affair with Wyeth has not weakened his position in Europe. On the contrary. He is perceived as a very honest business man. We need, in my opinion, this kind of leadership in business."[7]

Pfizer and Pharmacia Respond

None of that kind of support would help when it came to my future with Pfizer. Two weeks after my mail to Wyler Jennings I received his response: "We regret to inform you that there will not be a position for you in the new Pfizer organization."[8] He also wrote, "After the close, your job responsibilities will be the same as they are now until we notify you of a change."

This e-mail was clearly something several people had worked on and Wyler had simply sent off the final text. He hadn't even bothered signing his name. I felt the adrenaline rushing through my body and wondered how I was going to support my family. I realized that now I wasn't just going to have to continue my fight against Wyeth, I also had to challenge Pfizer.

What I knew was that if Wyler had stepped over the legal line in his prior e-mail, he had jumped miles over it with this one. Now he had told me outright that I would be terminated—after he had learned about even more legal issues. This was illegal both in New Jersey, where I worked, and in New York, where he worked.

The day after Wyler's message, I received a formal letter from Pharmacia's chief legal officer and general counsel. He mentioned that Pfizer had provided him with a copy of my e-mail to Wyler and stated that Pharmacia had conducted a "full legal review of the Genotropin franchise in the U.S.," and that, "as a result of the review a number of changes were made." He then admonished me for sending the letter to Pfizer and told me not to do this again "without the prior written approval of Pharmacia's Legal Department."[9]

SIX

The Private Detective

As part of my litigation with Wyeth, Wyeth's attorneys subpoenaed my Pharmacia personnel file, and I received a copy of these documents. Many of the e-mails and documents Pharmacia sent to Wyeth were generated by lawyers and could possibly have been withheld as part of attorney-client privilege. But apparently Pharmacia waived that privilege, which, to me, looked like an effort to help Wyeth in their defense against me.

The most amazing document of all was located neatly on top of a huge stack of papers. It was a file titled "Case Report, Case 2003-02-00003 Corporate, Pharmacia Corporate Security."[1] The date was interesting: The investigation had been started only a couple of days after I received the harsh admonition to keep quiet, from Pharmacia's general counsel.

My eyes nearly popped out of their sockets as I started reading:

> *Rost, Peter (CASE2003-02-00003)*
> *Category: Suspicious Activity*
> *Security Level: Corporate*
> *Status: Open*
> *Initial Description: Investigation of criminal/civil was commenced on Peter Rost. Also check to see if he purchased weapon in New Jersey.*
> *Requested By: Hardy, Basil*
> *Open Date: 2/6/03*
> *Review Completed: No*

I had never heard of Basil Hardy, so I looked him up on Pharmacia's intranet. He was head of Security. I turned the page and found a fax from "Rock Intl., Inc" with a post office box in Atlanta. The cover sheet indicated that the fax was fourteen pages long and said that, "Included in this fax are all the public records found on the database for Peter Rost. This includes assets as well as civil lawsuits, liens, judgments, and bankruptcies in New Jersey and Pennsylvania. He has California addresses associated with his name, although no public record information was found in California." The fax continued with two separate points. "The criminal records search was conducted— NO RECORD," and "Gun Permit—NJ—NO RECORD." Hand scribbled by Pharmacia's head of security was the sentence *"NO information to indicate a problem re violent behavior. 2/7/03, BH."*

There were reams of pages and faxes with personal data about me. Then I found a couple of handwritten pages from one of Pharmacia's human resource lawyers.[2] I had met with him to seek his assistance in talking to Pfizer a few days before the private detective had been hired. My meeting had apparently had the opposite effect of what I had expected. His notes left no doubt about how dangerous I was considered.

> *Rost—Basil Hardy*
> *1. Wyeth and time w/ US—Status of USA address?*
> *?to check—what else is going on??*
> *   Police?*
> *   Cases?*
> *2. Contacting—Wyeth Security counterpart ? to see NN*
> *harmful to self or others*
> *? address of Wyeth, get complaint*
> *3. Copies of emails w/ threats—to Basil*
> *? who's having daily contact??*
> *To let them know to notice and report unusual behav-*
> *ior/ any deterioration*

I had never seen anything like this before and I was truly shocked and appalled. I had gone from company high performer to security threat in a matter of days. This was something I couldn't have imagined in my wildest dreams. Pharmacia was a company that I had trusted—the fact that I had found illegal marketing and sales methods in my department didn't mean that I stopped trusting the entire corporation. But now, I felt as if I had been in a beautiful candlelit room, only to have a lightning flash suddenly reveal cracks, mold, and cobwebs. I just couldn't believe what I saw, and even worse, they had sent all this to Wyeth. All the loyalty I had felt to the company, all the respect I had had for executives in the organization vanished. And I was left with the ugly truth: I couldn't trust anyone. To even try to talk to them and reason with them was futile.

Psychoanalysis!?

But it got worse. As I flipped through the pages, I found more notes that Pharmacia's lawyer had written after I had spoken with him. The most sensitive parts were blocked out by a fat black marker, but what remained was astonishing in itself. According to his conclusions, I had no choices; I was out of a job with no likelihood of employment in the industry; I had every incentive to fight Pfizer, and he also claimed that I already hated them. This was news to me: I hardly knew Pfizer, but I certainly was reevaluating what I thought of Pharmacia after reading this. Then came the whopper—the notes implied that I might put a gun to my head so my family could get my life insurance.

All of a sudden I realized what a mistake I had made, trying to get help from a Pharmacia lawyer. I recalled that during our conversation he had suggested for me to contact the Employee Assistance Program. Perhaps this attitude shouldn't have been surprising; Pharmacia's lawyer clearly thought that anyone who tried to resolve potential criminal acts within the company *and* keep his job was a mental case.

The situation reminded me of dissidents in the former Soviet Union, who were hauled off by men in white coats to mental institutions. After all, if they didn't think communism was the best system in the world, they must be nuts, right? To my horror, I realized that the company I had respected and served for several years apparently had a similar philosophy. I had believed this company was different, I had been impressed by our executives, and now I felt betrayed.

At that point I vowed that I would expose the pharmaceutical industry and their methods. I would show the world what goes on behind closed doors and who these companies really are. But first, I had to fix the problems in my department. As the vice president of my franchise, I had to do everything in my power to correct things, or I could be next in line, accused of irregularities. And if I couldn't reason with Pharmacia or Pfizer, then maybe I could *force* them to take action. After reading those terrible notes I knew that they had not only misjudged me, they had also underestimated me.

There was more in that stack, sent courtesy of Pharmacia's legal department to aid in Wyeth's defense. I found heavily redacted, but partially readable, e-mails between Pharmacia's legal department and Pfizer's legal department. In one e-mail, a Pfizer lawyer forwarded the message Pfizer had sent to me, saying that I would be terminated. He asked Pharmacia, "Let me know if you guys have any more thoughts on this."[3] But for these e-mails I would not have known that the two companies were cooperating in their attack on me.

I read their e-mails and I vowed that they would never forget me. I would transform myself from one of the internal poster boys of a hard-charging healthcare hitman and loyal manager to someone who would show the world the dirty deeds of the industry I had worked for, for so long.

Reconnaissance

Pharmacia had hired their private detective, so I felt no hesitation when I started my own covert investigation. What I wanted to find out next was what Darren McAllister would say about me to future employers. As my direct supervisor, his support was crucial to get another job. Before taking on Pfizer, I needed to know what my options were, and if he was still loyal to me.

The fact that Darren had hired me not just once, but twice, was also important. First he had hired me into the international marketing department at Wyeth, in connection with the acquisition of the company I worked for at that time. Then he had hired me at Pharmacia and had repeatedly told me I had done a great job and was a candidate for "senior management." He had given me "thumbs up" after the Wyeth article was printed in the *New York Times*.

So I asked a recruiter with whom I was friendly to give Darren a call, just to find out where I stood with him.

The result of my little test came back in an e-mail:[4]

> *Dear Peter,*
>
> *I just spoke to Darren who is obviously a fan of yours. He was uncomfortable providing a reference without you having a specific offer in hand. He cited that the company recently re-enforced that they "strictly prohibit references" and that he needed to limit the conversation. He did offer that for 2002 that you "totally exceeded expectations on your performance review." I asked him if he would be a reference on your behalf at the time you do have an offer in hand and he said that "once outside the corporation, things could be different." I commented that he obviously thought you were quite talented because he hired you twice and he said "that's right."*

This wasn't entirely negative, but it was perfectly clear that Darren might decide to hide behind company policy. I now realized that I could trust no one any longer. Darren had been informed by Pharmacia's lawyers that I was a security threat. Of course, he wanted to distance himself.

Working for a corporation is like running with a wolf pack. Everyone helps out and is friendly as long as it benefits the group, but each wolf cares only about himself and will do anything to survive. Compassion, loyalty, caring, "best managed behaviors;" these are all buzz words invented to control the masses. If the ship goes down, the CEO leaves first on the biggest life boat with gold in his pockets, and his crew can fight over the remaining vessels and the weak perish. That is not so noble but it *is* corporate reality. I couldn't sit back and just be quiet.

Confronting Darren McAllister

I marched into Darren McAllister's office and dumped the file with the detective investigation in front of him. He put on his reading glasses and looked at the documents. Then he was quiet for a while, collecting his thoughts. He admitted that yes, they had asked him about me. He had told them that I was as stable as he could imagine and an utterly non-violent person. But he also took the company's side and said they had to be careful, they had a responsibility to other employees.

So I asked him directly, would he be able to recommend me when all of this was over? Darren hesitated and looked uncomfortable. After a while he said he would give me a reference, but that he would have to tell the next employer about my legal conflict with Wyeth.

"Why do you have to do that, it doesn't have anything to do with my job performance, does it?" I asked.

"I wouldn't feel comfortable not saying it."

"But you're not involved; you have nothing to say about it!"

"Perhaps, then, you shouldn't use me as a reference."

There it was, out in the open. Now I knew where he stood. I was not surprised but very disappointed. He had lauded my work, he had known me for many, many years, he had given me his thumbs up when he heard about the Wyeth situation, but none of that mattered anymore. The corporate isolation had started and I could sense the cold breeze. Just like someone from behind the Iron Curtain seeking refuge in the West used to become an Enemy of the State I had now become an *Enemy of the Corporation*.

Corporate Outlaw

The stack of documents Wyeth had received from Pharmacia contained more than just shocking revelations—I also read the praise other people had written about me when I joined the company. It felt like something from a bygone era, when I wasn't suspected of subversive activity. The irony is that one comment specifically mentioned that I had "high integrity."[5] None of these words, however, were going to help me get a new job. It became more important than ever to keep my position within Pfizer. Management had power, lawyers, and security people. I had only my own wits and my conviction that I could beat the corporate overlords at their own game.

SEVEN

The Investigation

PHARMACIA AND PFIZER HAD, TOGETHER, CAST THE FIRST STONE. It was time to defend myself. I didn't have any idea what Pfizer would do next, but I did believe that, just as in any fight, the one with the initiative holds the advantage. I decided to take a broad look at the corporate landscape before deciding my next move. I no longer felt nervous or anxious. I had to focus on the task ahead of me and I couldn't make a single mistake if I was going to survive.

If Pfizer had one weak spot, it was their bad conscience. Not necessarily Pfizer's own bad conscience; but the one they were about to inherit from Pharmacia. When a company buys another company, they also acquire all the liabilities. Not just financial liabilities, contracts, and other agreements, but also legal liabilities; liabilities for any misconduct. And by now Pfizer clearly knew they had issues with the endocrine-care business franchise.

My Response to Pharmacia

I decided to use the harsh letter Pharmacia's chief legal officer had sent me to open a dialogue, to get a feel for things. So I wrote a response in February 2003 and told him that I had a strong commitment to my franchise and the work we had done to clean up the business, but I also pointed out that while we had changed marketing and sales practices, this wouldn't release us from liability for what we had done in the past. I also informed him that Pfizer's threat to terminate me might violate New Jersey's whistleblower protection act. I ended my e-mail asking for his help to enlighten Pfizer in these matters.[1] To really kick up some dust, I also forwarded this e-mail to Ronald Chapman, Pfizer's general counsel and chief legal officer.

In the next round of documents Pharmacia delivered to Wyeth a few weeks later, I saw Ronald's reaction first-hand. His first mail to Pharmacia's chief legal officer asked, "What the heck is this all about?"[2] Pharmacia responded that I seemed to believe that by not offering me a job, Pfizer was unlawfully retaliating against me. Then Pharmacia's general counsel wrote, "I haven't done the research, but the theory seems dubious."[3]

This was *very* interesting. Pharmacia's most senior legal officer admitted that he hadn't checked the legal implications of the actions they had taken against me. They clearly didn't think I was all that important. While this is always a sobering realization, it also showed me how unprepared they were for dealing with an employee who actually knew some of his rights.

Exposure to Criminal Proceedings

It was time to pour more gasoline on the smoldering ashes of my career. Ronald Chapman probably had no idea that Pharmacia had delivered his e-mails to Wyeth's attorney, who was in turn obligated to turn them over to me. But I was happy to inform him of this. So I wrote him to say that I had reviewed his correspondence with Pharmacia's general counsel. I emphasized to Ronald that my situation was a simple employment matter, and his main concern should be his exposure to criminal and civil proceedings related to the endocrine care franchise.

I also made Ronald aware of Pharmacia's letter to me and wrote that based on the correspondence I had seen, he didn't appear to have been appropriately briefed on the situation in the endocrine care area.

I explained that I had been instructed not to communicate anything to Pfizer on this, but that I would be happy to meet with him. Of course, I realized that it would be a cold day in hell before he did any such thing.

Then followed the clincher—I stated, "You have based on this e-mail at a minimum been able to make an informed decision not to take any action. Should this result in any future adverse events there is now a written record that the responsibility for this decision was placed at the appropriate level in the Pfizer management structure."[4]

Unfortunately Pharmacia didn't deliver any more documents to Wyeth's attorneys, so I have no idea what kind of interesting correspondence ensued between Pfizer and Pharmacia. I did learn, however, that my message resulted in Pfizer taking one important action. They went out and hired the best law firm money could buy.

Time for Take-Over

The takeover date of April 17 approached rapidly. I sent a couple of last e-mails to my group, congratulating them for the incredible work they had done. Genotropin sales were bursting at the seams. Our sales came in 28 percent ahead of projections in the U.S., and our profit a whopping 74 percent ahead of expectations for the first quarter.[5] Our group had done a terrific job, and we hoped Pfizer would appreciate this. Fred Hassan even wrote one last e-mail to me, saying, "Congratulations to you and your team for global prescription business's role in this success."[6]

My boss—Darren McAllister—left Pharmacia on April 16, 2003, the day before Pfizer's takeover, and so did everyone else at his level. Pfizer didn't want anyone who could exert power or control from the old organization to remain on the premises. After the take-over, Pfizer started terminating Pharmacia employees in "waves," on a two-week schedule. Those of us in charge of our own departments soon found good use for our training in the art of firing people.

The whole situation reminded me of the scene in the epic movie *Spartacus*, in which the Romans forced the rebelling slaves to kill each other until there were none left. Pfizer didn't do the dirty work of terminating Pharmacia employees; they left that to Pharmacia managers, who later would be in line to be fired. At the same time, the ones joining the new Pfizer organization were whisked away to New York, leaving the condemned souls behind in New Jersey. Pharmacia's beautiful headquarters emptied rapidly. The people who attended their "separation" meetings said very little on the way out, especially to the press waiting outside. And we knew why.

The Secret Release Agreement

A leaked "Release Agreement"[7] circulated among Pharmacia's employees. This was a draft of the agreement departing employees had to sign in order to receive a severance package, which ranged from seven months up to a year's pay—more for some high earners and long-timers.

The agreement required that departing employees release and forever discharge the company from any and all claims in any way relating to their employment or termination. They also had to agree not to disclose the *existence* of the release agreement, including the amount they received for signing it. If they violated this term they had to return all the money paid to them, They also had to promise not to make any statements of a disparaging nature about Pfizer. Again, anyone in breach had to repay all the monies. Finally, the departing employees had to agree to cooperate in any potential or pending litigation that may involve them in any capacity, including meeting with Pfizer's attorneys, attending meetings, depositions, and trial, if necessary. Clearly Pfizer didn't want to take any chances. This clause would be one they would frequently exercise down the road, especially with the people in my group.

Saying Goodbye

On the day of the acquisition, I wrote the following to my department members: "As you set out on this new venture in your life I feel it is my responsibility as the department head for Endocrine Care to leave you with final words on the way." I attached an animated video of an alien singing "I Will Survive," only to be crushed by a giant disco ball. I liked to encourage a sense of humor about the impending disaster.[8]

I also sent a more serious mail, in which I asked everyone to extend the same commitment to Pfizer that they had to Pharmacia, and I told them that I would continue to lead the group until I was informed in writing that this was no longer the case.[9] I copied Wyler Jennings, Ronald Chapman, and a few others at Pfizer on this message.

Fortunately for me, Pfizer reacted to this mail. I soon got a response from Wyler, an e-mail I would have a lot of use for in the future. It said, "Thank you so much for your positive message to your group. I would like to clarify your reporting line. As you know Pfizer adopted a U.S. and a worldwide business model in the marketing group. Therefore, for the worldwide portion of your business, you are reporting to Harry Otter. For the U.S. portion of your business you are reporting to Ivana Fokker."[10]

Pfizer Brings In Reinforcements

Right after the e-mail from Wyler, I learned that Pfizer had hired Partland & Longhorn, one of the most prominent Washington law firms, to handle an internal investigation of my franchise. The firm was in a rush to see me. The day after the acquisition, someone from the legal department called and said that Lorenzo Ellenberg and his team from Partland & Longhorn wanted to meet with me.

Ellenberg was a partner in the firm, which consisted of more than 500 lawyers. He was in charge of their health-care practice group and had spent many years working on the type of issues I had brought to Pfizer's attention. He had a respectable background with the Justice Department, where he had coordinated several sensitive congressional investigations. Pfizer couldn't have hired better help. I was impressed.

Right before meeting with Ellenberg I sent another e-mail to Ronald Chapman and congratulated him on the selection of one of the finest firms and best attorneys in Washington, as well as for taking such swift action in response to my concerns. I told Ronald that I would recommend to Lorenzo Ellenberg that Pfizer approach the Justice Department and make a deal with them regarding the issues in my department. I also sent a copy of the e-mail to Lorenzo.[11]

Then I spent a full day with Lorenzo Ellenberg and his colleague, Pamela Berlin, from Partland & Longhorn's New York office. I was represented by my own lawyer, who declared from the beginning that he would plant himself like a flower in a pot and wouldn't disturb us much unless he got concerned about the questioning.

Lorenzo and Pamela were very efficient and went through every detail I had to tell them. They also wanted to know exactly who else in my department was aware of these details and later called in exactly the persons I had named. In spite of their professionalism, my sense was that Lorenzo was not very happy about what I was telling him. His attitude and tone were hostile and gave the impression that he already considered me an adversary, which surprised me a bit. At the end of the day I got the explanation. His very last question was if I had filed any suit, or contacted any government agency, related to any of the illegal matters I had discussed with him. Now I knew what he was really concerned about. I answered that I hadn't.

In the following days, many of my co-workers were interviewed. For the next year the Partland & Longhorn lawyers practically worked full-time with my team, asking them to turn over every piece of paper and every document they could find on Genotropin marketing and contacts with physicians.

Based on my meeting with Lorenzo and Pamela, I thought it was time to try to kick Pfizer's tires again.

An Admission

So I wrote to Lorenzo and suggested that he should have a good understanding of the issues associated with my franchise. But I also pointed out that so far, my efforts had not been met with any sign of appreciation from Pfizer, nor had they invited me to any key meetings or attempted to engage me in the continued management of my business. In fact, the only thing they used me for, during this time period, was to terminate my own people. I asked Lorenzo to inform Ronald Chapman that when someone is helpful, it is appropriate to say "Thank you." And I suggested that a senior manager at Pfizer would be welcome to do this. I also complained about the rather rude message from Wyler Jennings and suggested that, "It may at this time be appropriate for Pfizer to apologize for the disrespectful manner in which this mail communicated my pending termination." I also suggested that Pfizer might want to open a dialogue with me and reconsider their decision to terminate me.[12]

Finally, I pointed out how important a number of internal people were to the Genotropin franchise. I focused on the world renowned medical experts that Pharmacia had employed, and explained they were being offered demotions with Pfizer, and that this was insulting to them. (Unfortunately, Pfizer wouldn't listen and lost every one of these experts over the coming months.)

I had one last request in my letter. "I would think it is reasonable for Pfizer management to contact me . . . by June 1, 2003." I wanted to set a deadline to see how they reacted. I figured if they ignored me, they really didn't care, but if I could make them react, then they were concerned. I had absolutely nothing to lose.

By the end of May 2003, Lorenzo wrote me back to tell me, "I know Pfizer very much appreciates the assistance that you have provided."[13] A couple of weeks later, on June 9, I got a personal letter from Ronald Chapman.[14] What was most interesting was that it was dated May 28, 2003, which meant that it had either been sitting on his desk for ten days before he signed it, or he had backdated the letter to make it appear as if he had responded within the requested time line. Unfortunately it wasn't postmarked, since it was delivered through the internal mail system. The letter felt like a small ray of sunshine—maybe I had some leverage with Pfizer.

Ronald thanked me for taking the time to educate Pfizer and the lawyers about my business. He also wrote, "I recognize that, with your assistance, Pharmacia examined these issues in 2002 and made significant changes to correct the issues you raised."

This was good. Here I had a letter from the top legal officer at Pfizer, that I had indeed raised issues that warranted a change.

The letter continued, "Nevertheless, we are making additional changes to the endocrine care business based on our review, which we are also in the process of disclosing to the relevant government authorities."

This was even better. They had followed my advice to contact the government; this was also an admission that the issues I had brought to Pfizer's attention were serious enough to warrant government intervention. It meant that I had been right all along when I informed Pfizer of my discomfort with the limited changes Pharmacia's legal department had authorized. Most important was that he wrote the letter at all, indicating that I had some leverage. One question remained: Why was the date in the letter so out of sync with its arrival date?

Accusations of a Backdated Letter

I went on an info hunt, and it didn't take long until I found my next surprise. Back in 2001, thirty Nigerian families had sued Pfizer in federal court, saying the company conducted an unethical clinical trial of an antibiotic on their children.[15] The suit referred to a letter from the hospital saying the study had been approved by the ethics committee, and the suit claimed that Pfizer had *backdated the letter*. Moreover, a Pfizer infectious disease specialist had repeatedly told

Pfizer management that the company was violating international law and medical ethics standards. He was subsequently dismissed and later settled with the company, according to other newspaper reports. Clearly, the fact that Pfizer was accused of backdating one letter and that I might have received another one was significant. And so was the fact that they had fired one alleged whistleblower already.

Nine months after I received the May 2003 letter from Pfizer's general counsel, Pfizer's annual report contained the following statement: "The Company recently was notified that the U.S. Department of Justice is conducting an investigation relating to the marketing and sale of Genotropin and Bextra, as well as certain managed care payments. We are cooperating in these investigations."[16]

I didn't learn until later that Pfizer had been forced to sign not just one, but two Corporate Integrity Agreements with the Office of the Inspector General of the Health and Human Services (OIG), and they were obligated to report any misconduct, such as the issues I had brought up with them. The latest agreement is available to the public on the Health and Human Services Web site and states, "If Pfizer determines through any means that there is a Reportable Event, Pfizer shall notify OIG in writing within 30 days." The agreement defines a reportable event as, "anything that involves a matter . . . that a reasonable person would consider a probable violation of criminal, civil, or administrative laws." [17]

EIGHT

Sexual Liaisons

I HAD GIVEN PFIZER A GOOD LEGAL RATIONALE for not terminating or demoting me, but I had no reason to believe my position and salary remained secure. While I had received a civil letter from Pfizer's general counsel, my new bosses immediately made it clear that they didn't want to see me, and they completely cut me out of the business. In fact, they didn't call me or meet me even once after the April 2003 take-over. And when I sent an e-mail and suggested that we should have lunch, they didn't even respond. The fact that they were in New York and I was in New Jersey made it even easier for them to avoid me. Anyone they wanted to work with they relocated to New York, and the rest of us were left in New Jersey. We were the forgotten ones.

I didn't want to be forgotten any more than I wanted to be dismissed outright. And I knew that I couldn't let the company dictate the terms of our battle; a guerrilla force depended on speed and surprise. I was indeed a one-man guerrilla fighter, and I clearly could never win against the machinery of a $50 billion corporate war machine with 115,000 employees.

Powerful people are only afraid of losing three things, power, money, and reputation. I couldn't threaten their power; I couldn't take away their money; but I might be able to find a chink in their armor when it came to their reputation. And if they feared what I knew about them, they would be less prone to take away the lifeline I had left—my salary.

An Unusual Employee Survey

Given that I didn't have much to do anymore I had ample time to seek out Pfizer's weaknesses. As I searched the corporate intranet, I found exactly what I needed. Pfizer had done an exhaustive employee survey in 2001, and it was clear from the first page that CEO Hank McKinnell was proud about the fact that 88 percent of Pfizer's employees had responded.[1] There was lots of wonderful information about what Pfizer employees thought of the company; the highest ranked statement was, "I like working for Pfizer." A whopping 89 percent of the employees agreed with this sentence.

The second most favorable result was generated by the statement, "I am proud to work for Pfizer," a full 88 percent agreed with this. Only a contrarian might wonder why 12 percent weren't proud to work at Pfizer, or what those employees might have known about the company. At the time this survey was taken, 12 percent was equivalent to 6,000 employees.

But those weren't the numbers I was interested in. There was a different table in the survey that showed the lowest-ranked statements, and here things started to get interesting. The two most unfavorable ratings were given to the statements, "The right people get promoted," and "People are promoted for the right reasons." Only 36 percent and 42 percent agreed with these statements.

Soon I also discovered some data that didn't rank at the bottom, but still was a major red flag to anyone that cares about corporate ethics. Some 30 percent of Pfizer's employees, or about 15,000 persons at the time, didn't agree with the statement, "Senior management demonstrates honest, ethical behavior." And 34 percent didn't agree with, "I have confidence and trust in senior management." But the real surprise was that 49 percent didn't agree with the statement, "Management is willing to give up short-term gain to do the right thing." What was going on in Pfizer's executive suite?

What Pfizer's Employees Were Saying

It wasn't hard to make the connection with the rumors I had heard before the acquisition. Pfizer had a stellar public reputation, but what Pharmacia employees had been told by their Pfizer counterparts was something very different. This was a company managed by a group of people who had grown up together, partied together, and some of them had also allegedly spent time together between the sheets. What we heard was amazing—almost unbelievable.

I set out to find the truth. First I spoke to someone I knew well, an HR manager who had left Pfizer quite recently. He had spent many years working at Pfizer and believed the rumors were true—a group within Pfizer's management had been in and out of bed with each other for a number of years. In one instance a senior person allegedly dated a direct report while he was married. Soon after, that direct report turned and dated a guy reporting to *her*. And then this guy dated several women in his department.

The problem with this alleged situation was that it could create tensions if someone thought someone else received a favorable treatment because of sexual favors. Real or imagined, this is a situation that can't be tolerated by any management, since senior executives need to lead by example and can't be effective if they aren't respected, which, clearly, certain Pfizer executives were not.

An Insider's Story

I actually knew someone who had worked with the woman in one of these alleged relationships. We met over lunch and I asked him to confirm if the stories were true. He claimed that not only were the stories true, he had personally observed the woman and her subordinate touch and make loving gestures. He also said that their behavior had been embarrassing to other people who were in the same room as these two.

He explained how they'd had to make special arrangements when the female executive was dating her boss, whenever his wife appeared at corporate functions.

I realized that if any of this were true, it could cause a public meltdown of Pfizer's management team, much like the recent scandal at Boeing that had forced the CEO's resignation. I also sensed that if Pfizer knew that I knew, they might just handle me more carefully.

But I had a few concerns; I didn't want to expose any of the people who had helped me learn about this. Also, I knew firsthand how untrue such rumors can be. Finally, to bring up this kind of issue felt unsavory.

My Own Experience with Rumors

A couple of years earlier, when I had managed a region in Europe, I worked closely with a number of direct reports. One of them was a woman a few years older than I was. She was a force of nature, positive and outgoing. Some people apparently became jealous of her, and a rumor started to fly around that she was having an affair with me. I had no idea until she came to my office and told me, with tears in her eyes.

At first I almost laughed, it was so ridiculous. But then I realized that I'd better stop the rumor. So I delegated the situation to my HR director. She called the person believed to be the initial source of this misinformation; he had to fly to Stockholm from a different country. He had no foundation whatsoever for what he had said, and it appeared to be a case of speculation taking on its own life. We didn't terminate him, but he got the message and so did everyone else. My direct report was thankful, and as far as I knew, the rumors disappeared.

I wondered what to do in this current situation. I wanted to behave in an appropriate manner, while also keeping Pfizer off balance.

An Unusual Letter to Pfizer's CEO

On August 11, 2003, I completed mandatory training on "Pfizer Policies on Business Conduct," a course taught at the Pfizer Compliance Education Center. I decided to follow their instructions, to the letter. After much thinking, and many drafts, I wrote an e-mail to Hank McKinnell, Pfizer's CEO, as well as Ronald Chapman, Pfizer's general counsel.[2]

I started off by saying that my memo had been issued in accordance with Pfizer's recently issued "Open Door Policy" and "Pfizer Policy on Business Conduct." According to these policies, if you know of, or reasonably believe there is a violation of applicable laws or Pfizer's corporate policies and procedures, you must use the Open Door process to report that information to the Corporate Compliance Officer. I also reminded them that "it is strict Pfizer policy that no individual who raises an issue should suffer retaliation."

Then I informed them that several persons in Pfizer's organization had sought me out and disclosed the allegations in my e-mail and that they didn't want to come forward in a way that would allow Pfizer management to know their names. I also referred to Pfizer's guidelines on employment policies and the fact that the company advises its employees that they "should avoid situations that present either an actual or potential conflict of interest or even the appearance of a potential conflict of interest."

Having duly given them the context of my letter, I explained that employees had alleged that Pfizer management had violated the above guidelines by pursuing extramarital and other sexual relationships with people in their reporting line. This could create the appearance of a potential conflict of interest and there was also risk for an impact on employee selection and compensation if these liaisons had indeed taken place. Accepting sexual favors might clearly violate Pfizer's policy on conflict of interest.

Then I told them all the specifics about the various allegations.

I ended telling them that I was prepared to give detailed information, including dates, locations and facts related to the allegations listed in my memo. I also asked them to retain an independent law firm to investigate what I had brought to their attention.

I wrote the truth about exactly what I had been told, but I didn't know if the allegations themselves were true. That, however, wasn't the point. The fact that people thought they were true had eroded morale within Pfizer, as evidenced by Pfizer's own survey. As I looked over the e-mail, I was fairly sure that no Pfizer employee had ever had the audacity to give Hank this kind of information. And I have to admit that it took quite a bit of willpower to press the send button on my computer. It felt a bit like jumping off a cliff with a bungee-cord tied around my legs.

The Sex Investigation

I received a response almost immediately from Hank, "Thank you for writing. Your letter and allegations will be thoroughly investigated by our General Counsel, Ronald Chapman."[3]

Then Ronald wrote to me, "Our standard practice is for matters of this kind to be investigated, at least initially, by our corporate compliance group—a professional team of former prosecutors whose job is to provide thorough and independent evaluations of the matter."[4] Ronald also asked Arthur Richardson, Deputy Compliance Officer, to contact me and set up an appointment for an initial interview.

Based on Ronald's message it was clear to me that Pfizer didn't want to involve a third party. They wanted the information themselves. Arthur Richardson contacted me and told me he wanted to see me right away, together with one of his associates.

I went to his New York office the following day and met a very pleasant man. He had spent time as a prosecutor and the questioning was handled with utmost professionalism. Arthur and his partner wanted to know every detail I could tell them. By my assessment, they were completely unaware of all the talk that had been going on among Pfizer employees. This didn't surprise me, since senior executives and legal departments are for obvious reasons usually the last to find out what the rank and file employees are really saying.

But they also knew of the illegal marketing I had brought up, so they handled the situation according to the book. I emphasized that I had no first-hand knowledge about the situations I described; however, I convinced them Pfizer had, at a minimum, significant morale issues. Arthur and his colleague seemed most interested in the names of those individuals who had informed me of the alleged sexual activity, but I refused to give them to him.

Before the meeting ended I repeatedly asked them to hire an independent law firm that could shield the identities of the people who had given me this information. In response, they made it clear that was not "how they operated." They also discussed, and half laughed, about the impossibility of approaching the managers that were allegedly involved in these affairs. It was clear to me that they didn't think they could confront members of senior management. I wondered if they would have been so cautious if this had been, for example, a district manager having an affair with a sales rep or someone else further down in the power structure.

Too Hot to Touch

That same day, at eleven P.M., Arthur sent me a follow-up e-mail. He wrote that they lacked any details upon which to base an investigation. They had discussed the option of trying to track down the individuals with knowledge about the situation, but didn't expect that they would respond. He was also concerned that if they delved into specifics with third parties, they might risk harming the reputation of people, who, like all Pfizer colleagues, deserved to be treated fairly. He ended by saying that "these issues are never pleasant to deal with, and we appreciate your willingness to step forward and take what you believed to be the appropriate course, regardless of how difficult that course might be."[5]

I could understand the rationale for his arguments. It *was* tough to investigate. But why give up without trying? If they hired a third-party with assurances of confidentiality, people would most certainly talk. But if they investigated and came up with problems, they may have been forced to report this to the Office of the Inspector General, according to Pfizer's corporate integrity agreement.

By failing to find an avenue to investigate, they had avoided this potentially thorny problem. I couldn't let them off the hook that easily. So I asked what would happen if I did give them the names they wanted so badly. I'm not proud of that decision.

Pfizer's attorneys got interested right away. In a follow-up e-mail they said they wanted to "pursue this a little more."[6] They wanted the names badly, I could tell, and I just as badly wanted to believe that they were going to continue the investigation. So I told them—and I rationalized this to myself, thinking that the people I cared about had left Pfizer and the company couldn't hurt them. The others I didn't know too well and they would never have lifted a finger to help me, so why should I worry about their fate? I guess part of that "health-care hitman" attitude was still alive within me. The ends justified the means. I was fighting for my own continued existence, and I knew if I was any less ruthless than my opponent, I wouldn't make it.

I lost that bet. Pfizer never started an investigation,[7] so I gave up the names for nothing. I felt terrible then and I still do. As a result, there may be people who never see a promotion again within Pfizer, or worse, and they will never know the reason. Then again, perhaps Pfizer is a kind and caring company that doesn't judge anyone without a fair investigation, and those employees have nothing to fear. Pick the option you want to believe.

We had several more e-mail exchanges and talks, and I gave them more information. I was told that, in the end, they had decided not to pursue this matter so I put the situation out of my mind. That is, until a year and a half later, when I read the headline in the *New York Times*, "Boeing Chief Is Ousted after Admitting Affair."[8]

Boeing's Sex Affair

The chief executive of the Boeing Company, Harry C. Stonecipher, had been forced to resign after admitting to an affair with a female Boeing executive. His predecessor, Philip M. Condit, had also been forced to resign in 2003 because of ethical problems, including affairs with employees, and Mr. Stonecipher had come in to remedy these problems.

The *New York Times* reported, "The resignation was requested by Boeing's board after an investigation by internal and external lawyers." Lewis Platt, the chairman of Boeing, said that he had ordered the investigation after he received an anonymous tip. Mr. Stonecipher's resignation had been requested "because of actions inconsistent with Boeing's code of conduct, which reflected poorly on his judgment and would impair his ability to lead going forward."

According to *Business Week*, "Boeing Chairman Lewis Platt said allegations that Stonecipher had influenced the career or salary of the person with whom he had the affair had been investigated but proved to be unfounded."[9] This was all very interesting; because this was so similar to the possible implications of the allegations I had informed Pfizer's management of.

I immediately sent a copy of the *New York Times* article to Arthur Richardson and Ronald Chapman. I was sure it would jog their memory and perhaps lead to a reconsideration of hiring an independent law firm to investigate Pfizer's internal issues. To me this was an issue not about sex, but about corruption and a management willing to violate basic company guidelines.

Vanishing Questions and a Missing Survey

But there is more. In the summer of 2004, Pfizer conducted another employee survey,[10] similar to the one they did in 2001. I write "similar" because this time they removed all the embarrassing questions from the prior survey: What employees thought of Pfizer management and their morale.

Pfizer didn't stop there in their attempt to bury the embarrassing information from 2001. They also appear to have removed the old survey from their servers—at least I have not been able to find it again on Pfizer's intranet. Fortunately, I saved a hard copy.

NINE

Suicide?

GOING TO PFIZER WITH THE INFORMATION about affairs between superiors and subordinates hadn't been an easy decision. Talking about my sources was even harder. I knew—based on what had happened to my colleagues at Wyeth—that these situations can get completely out of control, making it impossible to predict who might get hurt.

I had recently learned that all those articles about my Wyeth lawsuit had had a devastating effect on many of my former colleagues. Because of the publicity, it could no longer be assumed that Wyeth was unaware of how their payment practices allowed underreporting of taxes in foreign countries, so Wyeth had finally been forced to take action.

I first heard about what happened in late March 2003, a few weeks before Pfizer was poised to take over Pharmacia. I was attending a business meeting and walking through the stylish lobby of the Mandarin Oriental Hotel, when my phone rang.

A Wyeth Executive with a Loaded Gun

The voice on the phone had a German accent, and it was a voice I remembered from what seemed like an eternity ago. There I sat—in the comfort of an orange sofa placed in a luxurious hotel lobby overlooking both the ocean and the Miami skyline.

The man on the phone cried and said that he had thought of killing himself. After the article ran in the *New York Times*, he and many others were ruined, he said. He would lose everything, and so would the others. I listened to him for over an hour as he told me his story.

He claimed that seventy-two employees in his country had been called to meetings with three lawyers sent out by Wyeth. All these employees had apparently received bonuses or other income paid from the U.S. over many years. The lawyers informed the employees that Wyeth would now report all this income to taxing authorities and they had two weeks, until April 14, to plead guilty to tax evasion to avoid criminal charges. He said that he had thought about suicide and that he had a 9 mm gun—a Luger—in his drawer, but that he couldn't force himself, since he had a family to think of. He also said that others had talked about suicide, too.

He said he knew what he had done was wrong, but that every-one—*everyone*—in senior management had done the same thing. It hadn't seemed so wrong at the time, with the exorbitant taxes his country charged. Then he started hinting at what he knew about other transactions that *he* could blow the whistle on.

Local corporate management in his country had been taken com-pletely by surprise by the tax raid, and he said they were running around like chickens without heads. He also told me of employees who had made mad dashes over the Swiss border to rearrange their Swiss bank accounts. Some could lose more than the money from Wyeth. Many had mixed that money with other funds they didn't want local tax authorities to know about. It was illegal to have a for-eign account in his country without notifying tax authorities.

I had no firsthand knowledge if any of this was true, but I cer-tainly knew the Swedish situation, in which even the managing director who took over my job later admitted to the press what had happened.

Troubling Press for Wyeth

As it turned out, 2003 wasn't a good press year for Wyeth. Not only did my tax story appear, but there were numerous other stories. Richard Carrion, who was a board member of Wyeth, and also chairman of Banco Popular de Puerto Rico, reached a deal in January 2003 with the Justice Department that his bank would pay $21.6 million in penalties to settle accusations that it laundered millions of dollars in drug money.[1]

Clifford Alexander, another Wyeth board member, was severely criticized in June 2003, in connection with his presence on WorldCom's board when that company fell apart—*USA Today* wrote, "Former WorldCom directors should get the boot from other boards because their credibility has been so damaged."[2] Later, Mr. Alexander along with other WorldCom board members had to pay investors $18 million from their own pockets as part of a legal settlement.[3]

And the CEO of Wyeth, Bob Essner, was featured in *Fortune* magazine in April 2003, as one of *Fortune's* 12 piggy offenders[4] in connection with a cover story with the headline "Have They No Shame?" The introduction to the article stated, "Their performance stank last year, yet most CEOs got paid more than ever."[5]

The Executive Who Lost $2 Million

But this particular story about what happened to Wyeth employees didn't stop there. Two years later, in 2005, I would encounter another old acquaintance, who had been one of the most senior officers of Wyeth Europe. She wrote me an e-mail and asked to see me in New York during her short visit to a pharmaceutical meeting. She didn't say what it was about, just that she wanted to see me. I was curious, wondering what she wanted to talk about.

We planned lunch together at her hotel, with a view of Central Park. She gave me a hug when she appeared. We got the best table next to the window, and, after the waiter brought water, she began to talk. She told me her husband had been killed in a car crash a year earlier. She didn't have any children, so now her work occupied all her time. It was what she lived for. They had moved her to Mexico, perhaps because of her language abilities, to oversee the Latin American region. She missed Europe, she said. Then she gave me a long gaze and got quiet.

I was feeling my way around and I figured that I better get the thing about my Wyeth lawsuit, which had alleged that international senior executives weren't paying taxes, out of the way. So I told her that I knew what she had gone through. And that I was really saddened. The waiter came with the food and we started to eat.

She nodded to me to continue, and I did. I observed her while I was talking and I felt her pain. I really liked and respected her. She was a generation older than me. And she had been almost like a matriarch to her people. Her people respected her.

My few words were all that she needed. She spent the rest of the lunch telling me what had happened. How the lawyers had come in and told everyone that they had two weeks to report their earnings to tax authorities. No chance to negotiate, and even the authorities had told her that they had never seen anything like that before: A large group of people self-reporting income that they hadn't declared for more than a decade back. She told me she had lost $2 million.

I just shook my head. "I'm so sorry," I said. "I'd like to say something more, but I really can't."

"I understand," she said. "I had to pay back 115 percent of what I made during those years—*115 percent.*" Her clear blue eyes looked sad and tired. "People lost everything." She named many names that I was familiar with, told me who had lost a house, who had lost even more than that. It was a terrifying tale.

I told her that when I was in Sweden, I had simply followed the advice of the company attorneys. I hadn't flipped out like some madman, set on suddenly changing how one company reported taxes. She nodded, took a sip of water, and said she understood. She wanted to know how the company had treated the people in Sweden. I said that

Wyeth had treated the situation very humanely.

She responded that this was what she had been told they would do with her region as well. But it didn't seem like she felt that is what had happened. She kept repeating that while she had lost most, many had lost what they didn't have anymore. They were old and wiped out. There was even a senior officer's widow who had known nothing and now, after her husband had passed away, found herself in the middle of a tax inquiry. She was bankrupted.

Many of the employees apparently had looked into taking legal action against the company and had hired lawyers. She asked what I thought of that. I responded that it wasn't something I could advise on.

Then she probed a bit further, saying that some of her colleagues talked about going to the press with what had happened. She asked if I would be interested in helping. I said no, I wasn't going to discuss anything about Wyeth with the press ever again. I wasn't sure of how interested she really was about going to the newspapers; it appeared to be more of another subtle test, to see where I stood. The meal ended and our time was up. I told her I had to go back to New Jersey. "You work in New Jersey?" she asked, "I thought you worked at Pfizer's headquarters here in New York. Did you come all the way in to see me?"

"Sure, I wouldn't have missed that opportunity to see you again."

An Executive Falls to His Death

A few weeks later, my eyes caught an unusual newspaper head-line. "Wyeth Executive Falls to His Death from Apartment." According to the article, the president of a Wyeth affiliate in a foreign country died on a Saturday night after slipping and falling from his 11th-floor apartment. The newspaper article said that the 57-year-old fell off the balcony's railing while tending to his potted plants. Detectives had also "ruled out the possibility that the executive was murdered, finding no signs of trauma on his body caused by external forces."[6]

The article went on to say that the man's wife and son were inside the apartment when the incident occurred. His family "said it was unlikely he committed suicide because he did not suffer from any psychological disabilities or financial difficulties and no suicide note was found."

I couldn't help but wonder if I had inadvertently caused this death through my legal actions. It felt strange—I felt a vague sadness, not much more. In a way, I was surprised that this was all I felt.

Perhaps it was the continued fighting that had left me drained, unable to truly feel anything. Or maybe I had become cynical about my fellow executives, knowing that very few of them would ever have stood up to do the right thing. Or maybe I was *just like* one of my opponents—ruthless and doing what I had to do to triumph, not worrying about the consequences. After all, I was fighting a personal war.

The fruits of war are death and destruction, but if we're not prepared to fight a war, we won't have peace. And I wanted peace.

TEN

Phone Surveillance

WHILE I WAS ADDRESSING RUMORS of improprieties with Pfizer's lawyers in September 2003, I was also dealing with Wyeth's lawyers and litigation. In a way, I was fortunate that Pfizer gave me so few responsibilities at work. It gave me time to focus on the Wyeth matter.

One day in October, Ed Silverman from New Jersey's *Star-Ledger* wrote a story headlined, "Wyeth and Former Executive Settle Suit."[1] I had nothing to do with this article. Ed had, in fact, called me once a week for several months to ask what was happening with the Wyeth situation. Each time, I told him "nothing new." Apparently he had approached Wyeth, since he wrote, "Wyeth and a former executive, who filed a whistleblower lawsuit against the drug maker, have reached a settlement, according to a company spokesman."

He continued, "The settlement ends an embarrassing episode for the Madison-based drug maker." A number of individuals on Wyeth's Yahoo message board picked up on this article. One was so funny that I forwarded it to Pfizer's management. It said "Former WYE executive now works for PFE!!! That tells me that PFE must be an ethical company!!!"[2] When I recently went back to check that message again, it had been deleted. But I had already saved it on my computer. Funny how many interesting documents and messages kept disappearing around me.

As October passed, the leaves outside my office window vanished, and so did my former coworkers, one by one. By the time the trees were barren, I only had one remaining employee reporting to me— my trusted assistant, who came in dutifully every day. By that time I started to show up at work only once a week. While I had a magnificent office, I didn't see any purpose in staring at my freshly painted walls all day.

Officially, I was still the vice president for the endocrine care franchise; Pfizer hadn't changed my title. And while Pfizer had written that, "After the close, your job responsibilities will be the same as they are now until we notify you of a change,"[3] I most definitely had nothing to do anymore. I was like the leader of a deserted island. Some of my cohabitants had perished; others had left in lifeboats. Now I and my trusted lieutenant remained, in permanent exile. No one called us, no one contacted us. It just remained eerily quiet.

Neither my assistant nor I had any idea of what to expect. But considering how sophisticated Pfizer had been in their psychological approach to Pharmacia's employees (getting them to open up and tell Pfizer all they needed, only to terminate them), there was no doubt in my mind that our isolation was another of their mental games. As long as they paid me, it would be harder to ask for damages in any claim I might have against them. The result was that I was like a corporate prisoner placed in a gilded cage, who didn't know the length of his sentence.

An Unusual Phone Call

What I didn't expect in the middle of this silent exile was a phone call from a former colleague. Jenna didn't have my direct number, so she had tried to call me through the switchboard in Peapack, where I worked. When she asked for me she said she got the third degree from the Pfizer operator.

The operator asked if she was a recruiter. She replied no. The operator then asked why she wanted to talk to me; she said she was an old friend. The operator then asked if she was a Pfizer employee; she responded no. The operator finally inquired about why Jenna wanted to talk to me. She replied that she was just catching up with me and was, at last, connected.

I had no idea the operator was screening my calls. What else might be happening? At the same time, this gave me an excellent opportunity to approach Pfizer again. I wrote an e-mail to Arthur, Pfizer's assistant compliance officer, and told him, in no uncertain terms, what had happened.[4] I also gave him Jenna's contact information so that he could verify the incident.

Arthur responded immediately: "I've never heard of this type of thing happening before. I'm looking into it."[5] He also wrote that it was possible that outside counsel—Partland & Longhorn—might have tried to pull my old e-mails related to the Genotropin issue. He added that usually e-mail purges make it difficult to study old e-mails.

More Surveillance

A few days later, I talked to some of the people in my old research group who now reported to a new manager within Pfizer. They told me that Pfizer had pulled cell phone and company telephone logs and that the lawyers had asked them questions about the content of those calls. I was also told that the lawyers had obtained their e-mails without their permission, which Pfizer policy allowed them to do. I realized that someone had probably snatched all my e-mails a long time ago.[6]

About six weeks later, I received a follow-up call from Arthur. He told me that my phone calls were being monitored; however, Pfizer had not initiated this. Phone monitoring was begun by Pharmacia and Arthur's compliance department had not been aware of this activity. He volunteered that Pharmacia had also put other people under surveillance. He explained that Pfizer's compliance department had placed several test calls to my phone, as well as to certain other individuals as part of their investigation.[7]

He was anxious to tell me that Pfizer had strong restrictions on these kinds of monitoring activities and did not do this outside the scope of specific investigations, unless requested by law enforcement or if someone was deemed dangerous, "which you are not," he added helpfully. He also said he would immediately contact the supervisor for Pfizer's Peapack switchboard and stop this practice. Pfizer was retreating, and my questions were clearly keeping them off balance.

Arthur admitted that e-mails might have been pulled from my mailbox related to the Genotropin investigation. He said they did this based on a key word search and explained that no ongoing search of my e-mails unrelated to this investigation should exist. Finally, he reiterated that they had not found an "avenue to investigate" the issues I had raised related to senior Pfizer management. Surprising even myself, I found that I believed Arthur Richardson. His tone and the level of detail of the information he provided indicated that he was speaking the truth. I couldn't help it—I liked the guy.

I had a lot to think about at this point; however, I never expected to have to question what Arthur had told me. The phone monitoring didn't stop. The following year, in 2004, my assistant told me that a recruiter had tried to reach me and had had difficulty getting through.

Another Strange Call

I spoke to the recruiter later in the day and I asked her where she had called and what the operator had said. The recruiter told me she had called Pfizer in New York, they had asked what her name was and the reason she wanted to talk to me, as well as some other questions.

"This happens all the time," she said.

"Does this happen with all the pharmaceutical companies?" I asked.

"No, only with Pfizer. No one else does this."

I asked her why she thought Pfizer did this, and she responded that based on the questions she had received she thought they recorded the information.[8]

Later in the fall of 2004, when I began to speak out publicly in favor of drug reimportation and journalists called me at work, Pfizer's operators completely refused to connect my calls, and instead referred callers to the public relations department.

When I learned about this new development I decided to call and ask for myself. It was a pretty funny experience. First, the operator asked whom I wanted to talk to. When I answered she said okay, but then there was silence for a few seconds. Then she came back on the phone and asked why I wanted to talk to Peter Rost. I said it was a private call. She didn't accept this and wanted to know my name. I responded truthfully, "Peter Rost." So she said, no—she wanted to know *my* name. I said that my name *was* Peter Rost.

Now she was really confused and told me again that my name wasn't Peter Rost—that was the person I wanted to talk to. So I told her I wanted to talk to myself. Now she probably thought this was some practical joke, so I explained to her that I was, indeed, Peter Rost, and I had called to check what she did.

And now I wanted to know why she didn't let me through. She said Pfizer screened all calls for vice presidents. That was certainly very different information than what I had received from Arthur.

The system wasn't fool-proof. A few nice operators sometimes did let calls through. Also, I was told by some callers that a few in Pfizer's public relations department appeared sympathetic to my cause and had supplied them with my private number.

ELEVEN

Fake Numbers

PARTLAND & LONGHORN HAD WORKED FOR NINE MONTHS on the investigation of the illegal marketing issues that I had brought to Pfizer's attention when they suddenly contacted me again. Now they wanted all my business files. It was December 2003, only a few days before Christmas, and it surprised me that it had taken them so long to request this. I knew that they had spent the fall poring over every document they could find in my old department and interviewed people over and over again. Now, I guess, they thought it was time to see what else I might know.

Over the holidays, I sat down and went through all the files in my office cabinet. As I did so, I had a hard time believing someone hadn't already copied all those documents surreptitiously. I only had about two boxes of documents. I asked my assistant to copy and pack everything. But, when I decided to go through the files one last time before she sent the whole thing off, I discovered a set of documents that I had all but forgotten. Based on the gravity of these documents, that might seem surprising, unless you take into account that all of 2003 had been spent fighting to keep my job and looking at marketing violations.

Following the Numbers Trail

Back in the spring of 2002—a few months before the take-over announcement and a year before Pfizer's actual acquisition of Pharmacia—I had discovered something that greatly worried me. Reviewing the monthly financial numbers of Genotropin sales at various international affiliates, I noticed that our market share in Japan—our largest market outside the U.S.—was completely flat. Not just for a few months, but year after year. That, however, wasn't what worried me most.

What caught my eye was that in spite of this flat market share, our sales kept increasing. Additionally, the overall market was *decreasing*, due to mandatory price reductions. So I had started to suspect that my Japanese colleagues were playing around with their numbers, most likely by inflating sales by loading in product to distributors and wholesalers.

Perhaps the biggest reason for my worry was that Japan was Pharmacia's biggest affiliate and Genotropin the largest product in that market. If the numbers were being doctored it could have major impact on not just my franchise, but also on Pharmacia. The second reason I was concerned was that my bonus was partly determined by how well local markets met their forecasts. I didn't want to be in a situation in which sales got more and more inflated year after year, and suddenly the bubble burst on my watch. The year that bubble broke, my personal bonus would be severely impacted.

And then there were the questions about legalities.

When we had talked to our colleagues in Japan we hadn't gotten any answers that made sense. So I had set out to covertly investigate what was going on. I put one of my best employees on the job—Isadora Pelozzi—the same person Pfizer would later retract their job offer from. She started digging and spent a lot of time with our Japanese counterparts, looking at sales trends and wholesaler inventory, and she scrutinized financial statements.

On July 1, 2002, Isadora came to me with a slide presentation. Based on her information, I could see how each December they had increased their load-in of sales—basically selling much more in that month than in the other months. So each year they took some of the sales that really belonged in the following year, to prop up their numbers. This, of course, is a Ponzi scheme, doomed to fall apart when there aren't enough sales to move over. I also foresaw that they would need an even bigger load-in in 2002 to make their numbers.

There was no question about what to do. I wanted to have everything in writing, so I forwarded Isadora's presentation to Darren, my supervisor. I wrote, "Attached presentation confirms the discussion I had with you about Japan. Basically our market share is steady. Forecasts, however, last year, this year, and possibly in the future are higher than the market can generate. This resulted in a higher December 2001 load-in than December 2000, and if things continue this way, will lead to even higher load-in 2002. We need to understand how far management is willing to push this."[1]

I continued with several additional concerns about how Japan managed their profit & loss statement and their expenses, and I ended the memo in the harshest way possible, "Without appropriate additional information you cannot use Japan P&L to judge performance of your team, nor can you use this to determine incentive levels. The same situation may exist in Europe." I wrote this because I had also looked at the financial spreadsheets for Europe and found some suspicious sales developments that didn't appear to reflect market trends.

Please note that I was investigating all this before the downfall of Enron and WorldCom, and before Bristol-Myers Squibb pleaded guilty to stuffing the channels in 2004. I took what, now, seems to be a low-key approach to the problems. My worry at that time was my bonus and the fact that some renegade affiliates might be playing fast and loose with their numbers. I didn't know that companies would actually go belly up and CEO's would go to jail because of this kind of behavior. Darren told me that he would contact his superiors regarding this matter. After that, I didn't hear a word more about this issue from anyone at Pharmacia.

High Pharmacia Inventories

As I reviewed my old documents, I decided to take a look at what I could find on the net. If this were widespread within Pharmacia, it might have left marks in other areas, marks that Pfizer would be in a rush to erase. And it didn't take long until I found what I was looking for.

In one of Pfizer's financial filings in January 2004, I read that, "For 2003, the harmonization of Pfizer's and Pharmacia's accounting and operating practices negatively impacted full-year revenues by approximately $500 million and diluted EPS (earnings per share) by $.07. The principal factor was the reduction of legacy Pharmacia wholesale trade inventories, which has been completed."[2]

Whoa! I thought. *That's a serious impact.*

Then I found an article from the Associated Press, which announced, "Pharmacia Inventory Cuts Pfizer Earnings," and said that the reduction of inventory levels at the former Pharmacia would knock 7 cents a share off Pfizer's 2003 earnings, according to Chief Financial Officer Gideon Braxton. The article also said, "When Pfizer bought Pharmacia, Pharmacia had products sitting on wholesaler's shelves for an average of 2.2 months. Pfizer's products, which include Viagra and Lipitor, sit on wholesalers' shelves for an average of 0.8 months."[3] That is a *big* difference.

So What Is The Problem?

Usually executives need to grow sales 5–10 percent in a fiscal year to earn a bonus. But let's assume they can't meet their own forecasts and they decide to sell more products to the wholesalers (who distribute to pharmacies) than the market can bear, to make it look as if sales increased. The wholesaler, however, can't sell all its inventory to the pharmacy, so wholesaler inventory increases.

What the numbers above proved was that Pharmacia had a wholesaler stock level that was more than twice as high as the one

Pfizer thought necessary to have enough products for their customers. In fact, Pharmacia's inventory level was, according to this report, 1.4 months of sales higher (2.2–0.8 months). On an annual sales basis that is equivalent to 1.4/12=11.7 percent of annual sales. If this so-called "channel stuffing" hadn't taken place, Pharmacia's past sales increases would have been almost 11.7 percentage units lower. Since Pharmacia's management got incentive payouts based on sales from the company to the wholesalers, clearly some executives had made a lot of money on this high inventory level.

So my suspicions had been right on the money. It wasn't just Japan. In fact, someone at Pharmacia had pumped up wholesale inventories to levels where Pfizer felt it was appropriate to take one-time charges and start over again. But my understanding was that these charges only applied to U.S. operations. I wondered how much had been going on outside the U.S.

What I had in my own documents might be the smoking gun which indicated that Pharmacia had done the same thing overseas, in their largest market. This could mean that Pharmacia's accounting was questionable, and perhaps Pfizer had overpaid for the company. But since Pfizer now owned Pharmacia and didn't want to be second-guessed about their deal, this was not something they would be excited to reveal to investors. As I sent my files off to the lawyers at Partland & Longhorn, I wondered what would happen next.

TWELVE

The Big Surprise

IN OUR PRIVATE STATE OF EXILE, my secretary arrived faithfully at the office each morning and stayed all day, every day, in spite of having virtually nothing to do. She had become quite good friends with the moving coordinators. In January 2004, she told me that she had heard Pfizer was about to move our offices again. If true, this was going to be our third move in less than six months.

I didn't mind my most recent office space. It was a beautiful building with large offices; mine even had a tray ceiling. Unfortunately, Pfizer planned to convert the whole thing to cubicles and wanted to cram more people into the building. No surprise there, but it meant I would have to move again and that had really become a hassle. I wondered whether they moved me around to make life uncomfortable. My secretary told me she had spoken to the vice president of operations at Pfizer. He told her that, "HQ knows who you are and that you're here." She was very surprised about that remark, since she didn't know any of the legalities I was involved in.

The Sarbanes-Oxley Act

I figured it was time to do some more research, this time to find out if moving people repeatedly was something Pfizer could really do. Again, it didn't take long until I found what I was looking for. In an article in *CFO* magazine called "The Untouchables," I discovered the following advice: "Even changing someone's cubicle location or reassigning him or her to a different client or project may be construed as retaliation."[1]

It also said that, "Whistle-blowers who report suspected violations of securities laws now have broad protections under the Sarbanes-Oxley Act of 2002—so broad, says employment attorney Michael Nosler of Denver-based Rothgerber Johnson & Lyons LLP, that companies should treat any employee who voices a concern with kid gloves."

I had never heard of the Sarbanes-Oxley Act, but I was intent on learning as much as possible about this new area. A quick bit of research left me quite impressed.

On July 30, 2002, President Bush signed into law the Sarbanes-Oxley Act, which had been written in response to the many recent corporate scandals. The act not only gave financial whistleblowers protection, it also made retaliation against certain whistleblowers a felony. The beauty was that the new law amended the chapter of the criminal code that dealt with obstruction of justice and specifically changed a section addressing witness tampering.

The new section provided that, "Whoever knowingly, with the intent to retaliate, takes any action harmful to any person, including interference with the lawful employment or livelihood of any person, for providing to a law enforcement officer any truthful information relating to the commission or possible commission of any Federal offense, shall be fined under this title or imprisoned not more than 10 years, or both."[2]

For employers, the new statute "is disastrous in terms of its broad coverage," *CFO* magazine wrote. In my case, the Sarbanes-Oxley Act appeared to fit hand in glove with the accounting issues I had discovered in Japan.

And not only had the new law provided for criminal penalties for certain types of retaliation, it also stipulated civil penalties. The Act protected employees who take "lawful acts" to disclose information or otherwise assist criminal investigators, federal regulators, Congress, or the employee's supervisors. Protection is given under the new law as long as the employee "reasonably believes" the employer's conduct is a violation of federal securities law, even if the questioned conduct is later determined to be lawful.

I realized that I had already given Partland & Longhorn documents that would place me under the umbrella protection of this act, but I needed to be able to *prove* that I had actually done so. It was time to write another letter to my legal friends, who had already billed Pfizer for so many hours over the past year. But in writing the letter, I was able to bring to light yet another issue that had recently caught my interest.

In January 2004, I had dinner with Isadora Pelozzi and a few old friends from Pharmacia. We were seated around the table in the kitchen of a former co-worker with Indian take-out food and plenty of beer. The Japan situation had been on my mind, because of the documents I had rediscovered, and I reminded Isadora of the research she had conducted to find out if our Japanese colleagues had stuffed the channels with Genotropin. Isadora told me that not only did she think that Japan stuffed the channels, but she had also been told that they had paid their wholesalers to take on the extra stock.

I was a bit dismayed that I hadn't been told about this earlier but happy that I found out now. This was *major* news to me. It meant that Japan had done exactly what Bristol Myers-Squibb had been caught doing—paying wholesalers to take on more product than they could sell, simply to make the sales numbers look better. Isadora also told me that the Japanese affiliate had accounted for this kickback as an expense the following year.

During our discussion, we calculated that it was possible that Japan might have inappropriately accounted for $20–25 million in sales for Genotropin. It could mean that if Pharmacia had done this on a global scale for more products in countries outside the U.S., the total amount could be up to $500 million. An additional $500 million, related to overstocked U.S. wholesalers, was what Pfizer had already listed in their 8-K report.

So in total it could be close to a $1 billion problem, a pretty serious number when one considers that Pharmacia's total sales for the last full year they were in business was around $14 billion. It was an even more dire number if one considers the following: The year before Pfizer took over Pharmacia, sales increased by less than $200 million. The year before that, the sales increase had been around $1 billion. If Pharmacia had done all this wholesaler-stuffing, then their sales had not increased much, if at all. That, in turn, would mean that all those fantastic bonuses Pharmacia's executives received weren't warranted. And more important, the company itself may have been significantly overvalued.

Only a formal investigation could verify or dismiss my concerns. Just the same, I summarized the situation in an e-mail to Pamela and Lorenzo at Partland & Longhorn and copied Wyler Jennings and Ronald Chapman. I ended my letter by saying, "If Isadora's information is correct and if inappropriate load-ins were systematically implemented ex-U.S. to enhance sales performance, in addition to the high Pharmacia wholesale trade inventories already disclosed by Pfizer, this may have implications under the Sarbanes-Oxley Act."[3]

It didn't take long until I heard from Pfizer's lawyers. Now they didn't just want me to come in for another full-day meeting, they wanted me to turn over my laptop to the IT department. They were not sure that a prior "download was completely successful in capturing everything on the laptop."[4] They were especially interested in getting the e-mails on my computer.

THIRTEEN

The SEC Gets Involved

PRIOR TO THE PLANNED MEETING with Partland & Longhorn, I sent Pamela a FedEx of old e-mails and memos that I had printed out and saved over the last few years, memos that showed in chronological order what had happened during my interaction with Pfizer and Partland & Longhorn. I included an e-mail from my assistant complaining about our multiple moves, the article from *CFO* magazine,[1] and an alert about the Sarbanes-Oxley Act, covering the criminal statute for retaliation.[2]

Both Lorenzo and Pamela attended the meeting, which took place in the Partland & Longhorn offices in New York. It was a typical New York law office, with long, softly lit corridors, a highly professional receptionist, people speaking in hushed voices, and lots of dark wood furniture.

As I arrived and sat down at the large conference table, I noted that both Pamela and Lorenzo had a big, black binder in front of them. The binders didn't say "The Big, Black, Peter Rost Binder" on their spine, but they could just as well have, for as they flipped through them, I recognized all my documents.

To my great satisfaction, I also noted that the first document behind one of the tabs was the Sarbanes-Oxley page, detailing criminal penalties for retaliation against someone who informed a law enforcement officer of an offense, and the article about not moving people who had blown the whistle. They had clearly gotten the message.

I figured the true test would be if they moved our offices again or let us stay put. Just to keep you from guessing, I will tell you what happened right away: Pfizer blinked. A few weeks later, they moved the entire research group to dinky, old offices far away from the Peapack facility, but they left me and my assistant alone. We even remained in the building as workers in hardhats started tearing down the offices around us. At that point, we were the only two people left in the entire building.

This cessation of movement gave me a rare insight into how concerned Pfizer really was about my case. They probably didn't even realize that I was less worried about having my office moved than I was interested in their reaction. Our isolation in an empty building continued for six more months, until my assistant resigned and finally Pfizer moved me out to complete the renovation of the building. In the summer of 2004 they gave me another very nice office—a corner office right next to corporate security.

The Memo Pfizer Didn't Like

But back to my interview with Pfizer's lawyers: The first thing they wanted to know was whether I could tell them anything else that I hadn't already informed them of. Fair enough. They clearly feared that I would let them know about possible violations in bits and pieces over the years to come, holding them hostage, so to speak. Nothing could have been further from the truth, and I told them so, saying that I had nothing more than the Japan situation to discuss.

According to the *National Law Journal*, the billing rate for partners at Partland & Longhorn range from $325 to $600 per hour.[3] This is pretty much standard in big cities. As Pamela and Lorenzo added hour after billable hour to their firm's income, I felt more uncomfortable than I had at any of the prior interviews. They appeared to be much more interested in what I *didn't* know than what I knew. It was weird and I suspected they were trying to cover up something.

So to make sure that it wasn't just the Partland & Longhorn lawyers who documented what I had said during our meeting, I wrote my own summary of concerns to Pfizer's management. That way there would be no doubt about what I knew and what the financial issues were.

Three days later I sent my memo to Gideon Braxton, Pfizer's chief financial officer, and Ronald Chapman, Pfizer's general counsel. I wrote that if the information I gave Partland & Longhorn on March 9, 2004 was correct, Genotropin in Japan may have experienced a significant increase of wholesaler inventories over several years. Sales incentives had allegedly been offered by Pharmacia Japan to its wholesalers at the end of a year, in order to encourage wholesalers to buy an amount that would help Pharmacia meet their annual sales projections. If this was true, it might force Pfizer to restate its sales and earnings results.

I also pointed out two possible "material weaknesses" (these are defined under standards created by the American Institute of Certified Public Accountants) relating to Pharmacia accounting and public financial reporting. The first problem was that the incentive may not have been accounted for in the correct year, since it was allegedly given one year and expensed the following year. The second problem was that under generally accepted accounting principles, it might not be appropriate to recognize sales resulting from these incentives, until the wholesalers had actually sold the additional supply.

I ended my memo by suggesting that if Pfizer verified the alleged wholesaler inventory buildup, they might want to take steps to strengthen internal control processes so that they could identify and rectify any additional accounting errors in other businesses or geographic areas.[4]

The Angry Response

After almost two weeks had passed, Pamela responded in one of the most hostile letters I have ever received.[5] In short, Pfizer, through their lawyers, attempted to tear apart every sentence in the e-mail I had sent, and the lawyers tried to use my comments during our meeting to somehow prove that what I had written wasn't true. To me this was surreal and confirmed my suspicions that something was very wrong: They didn't have to argue their defense with me, I simply wanted to notify them of a potential problem. Clearly they weren't interested.

Additionally, they certainly didn't like the most recent documents I had sent them. Pamela continued her letter, "You recently provided Partland & Longhorn with a file purporting to be a Pharmacia business file (which we had requested) but which, in fact turns out to be your own perceived road map for threatening whistleblower suits." The fact that the business documents I had turned over would help me in a whistleblower suit was completely true, so perhaps it wasn't surprising that they were so upset when they discovered this material.

I responded by explaining in detail the accounting issues with numerous examples. I also told them that I was taken aback by the content and tone in their e-mail, and I made it clear that, based on their response, I didn't think they had any intention of objectively investigating the accounting issues I had brought to their attention. Because of this I felt that I had no choice but to notify the SEC.[6]

I also wrote that their statements gave the impression that they had not taken advantage of the considerable legal resources within Partland & Longhorn and I urged them to do so.

That same day, I expressed my concerns in an e-mail to the SEC. The SEC responded by opening an investigation less than twenty-four hours after they received this material. A number of my former colleagues were subsequently called in to be interviewed. All of this could have been avoided if Pfizer and their team of lawyers had shown a minimum of willingness to investigate their internal accounting situation. It only surprised me that I never saw Pfizer write a word about this investigation in their quarterly report, the way corporations normally disclose government investigations and other material events to their investors.

FOURTEEN

You Will Never, Ever Work Again

SPEAKING OUT IS A DIFFICULT THING TO DO. If an employee who has been harmed does that, he is immediately blacklisted. My case was no different, and I had a good way of measuring its effect. During the time when Pfizer was about to take over Pharmacia, recruiters circled around Pharmacia employees like bees around honey. Most of us received many phone calls every week from someone looking to fill a particular position. Often there wasn't even a close fit, but they kept calling.

I received my fair share of calls and even had some interviews set up. Those interviews, however, came to an abrupt halt as soon as my lawsuit against Wyeth was made public in the *New York Times*. It was almost comical to hear the excuses people gave.

The most memorable situation was a biotech company that had begged for me to see them. The recruiter had worked as head of personnel at a company I had once worked for and knew me well; the president had been the CEO at the same company; and one of the board members had been my direct supervisor and had known me for many years. They had repeatedly asked me to come and interview, and I had agreed, even though the role was more limited than my current position.

It didn't take more than a couple of days after the *New York Times* article for the recruiter to call and say they had put the new position on hold. I was a bit suspicious, so I called the company to check the situation. First I spoke to the assistant to the president. She let it slip that the position wasn't on hold, that it was just "me." I then called the recruiter back and he said she didn't know what she was talking about.

This wasn't the only case of someone suddenly losing interest in me. A friend told me she had spoken to the recruiting firm who had assisted in hiring me in the past, and they had told her that I would never work in the pharmaceutical industry again, and that "it was a real shame for such a talented guy." Their prediction didn't take long to be confirmed. The number of calls I got from recruiters slowed to a trickle until they all but stopped. Of course, it didn't help that Pfizer later put the brakes on who could reach me.

But even if I had been given another job offer, I had one more problem to deal with. That was whether Darren, who now worked at Schering-Plough, would ever give me a reference. When I had pressured him before he left Pharmacia, he had confessed that he was concerned of what Gertrude and Fred would say if he helped me, and that he hoped to go to work for them. Now he *was* working for them, and I wondered if his concern remained now that he was safely employed. All I asked, in fact, was that he simply be honest and objective about my performance at Pharmacia and stand by what he had written in my performance reviews.

Hiring My Own Detectives

To test Darren's behavior, I decided to use a reference-checking service. I felt a little bit sneaky about using such a firm with someone I had known for many years, someone I had liked and trusted, but I figured that I didn't have much of a choice. It took over six weeks for the reference checking service to complete their job. I had been told by colleagues that Darren was giving references to many of them, so I couldn't wait to hear what he would—or wouldn't—say about me. When I received the summary of the report I lifted an eyebrow.

Darren had proven that years of hard work for him, great perform-ance ratings, and the fact that he had hired me twice meant nothing. This is what the reference service wrote:[1]

> We've made numerous (8 plus) attempts to contact your reference but they are not returning our mes-sages. We must be very cautious with your reference. If there are too many calls made it may signal to your reference that something is amiss. Any potential employer would call no more than 2 times and at that point they would dismiss this reference as not wishing to give a reference.
>
> It is our opinion that we must discontinue the refer-ence checking process and close your order as not to look suspicious or unnatural to your caller. The last thing you would want would be that your reference believes a potential employer or you are harassing them. Please look at this situation as a potential employer would; obviously this reference does not care to respond, thus implying that they do not want to give you a good reference. The mere fact that they are not returning the call does imply that they do not wish to discuss your previous employment. [1]

Darren was my most important reference, from my most recent job. If he refused to respond, I would be locked out of any future job. I pulled out my last Pharmacia performance appraisal. It was dated November 18, 2002. At the end Darren had signed his name:

> The condensed comments above cannot entirely reflect the tremendous difference Peter's leadership has brought to the department. He has effected a major reorganization, has reanalyzed many aspects of

the business with a zero-based approach, and essentially rebuilt plans from the ground up. His significant role and the energy he has devoted will pay off even more in the future. Peter is a key leader with potential for an even larger senior Marketing role or a high-level role within Operations.

Darren ended the appraisal giving me an "Exceeds Expectations" rating on the quantitative assessment, qualitative assessment, and the overall assessment.[2]

Nothing like a Good Lawyer

Darren's decision made it even more important for me to keep my job with Pfizer, however absurd my situation with them remained. I was feeding and sheltering my family, but that was about it. I had no career and mounting concern over what would happen next. Pfizer had, in their recent and very hostile communication related to the accounting issues I had brought to their attention, for the first time in a year repeated that I wouldn't have a future with Pfizer. They had explained that the reason I still had a job was that "Pfizer policy provides that when an employee scheduled to be separated raises compliance issues, the departure is put on hold until an investigation of the claim is completed."[3]

Since Pfizer hadn't changed their mind and I was locked out of the pharmaceutical job market, I realized that I needed some good advice. So I called one of the lawyers who had helped me get the Wyeth suit "dismissed to the mutual satisfaction of both parties." The lawyer's name was Jon Green and he had the reputation of being one of the sharpest employment litigators in New Jersey. He only worked with wronged employees, never for corporations. I once asked him why, and he said "because I don't have the stomach to represent guilty companies."

Jon Green had just left the law firm where I had met him and started a new firm in central New Jersey together with two of the other lawyers. Both Jon and his partners had stood as counsel in a number of ground-breaking decisions that had expanded employee legal rights and were actively involved in publishing articles and lecturing both locally and nationally on employment-law. He was, without doubt, one of the best employment lawyers on the East Coast, and his firm had received the highest rating from the legal peer-rating system maintained by Martindale-Hubbell, so I knew I was in good hands with him.

He didn't fear the big guys and had successfully challenged many powerful opponents, including companies such as AT&T, IBM, Verizon, Mercedes-Benz, Nieman Marcus, and Exxon-Mobil.

I have to admit, however, that I had learned a long time ago to follow my own instincts at times. That meant I expected to give Jon the occasional virtual heart attack with my *ad hoc* interactions with Pfizer. I was sure he would enjoy the ride, though, and felt most thankful when he took me on as a client again. In doing so, he said that he had never had a client like me before, and it didn't sound as if he necessarily wanted more of my kind. I, no doubt, livened up his practice. Jon was the perfect lawyer for me.

Jon's Letter to Pfizer

Jon knew every wrinkle in New Jersey's employment law, every verb that could backfire, and every out an employer could try. He soon discovered some important facts that would work in my favor. He also alerted me that, for some laws and claims, there was a risk that the time to file a complaint was running out, and that we needed an agreement with Pfizer, otherwise we would have to sue them right away. So he sent a very important letter to Pfizer. He described the various events I had experienced, and then concluded:[4]

Thus, the illegal conduct that Dr. Rost raised during the October 28, 2002 meeting not only constitutes protected activity under the New Jersey Conscientious Protection Act but also pre-dates the January 17, 2003 e-mail from Wyler Jennings that informed him that Pfizer would not offer him one particular VP position, claiming that he understood that was the only type of position that Dr. Rost was interested in, in spite of no such limitation having been communicated by Dr. Rost. Mr. Jennings's January 17 e-mail was sent late Friday evening, on the same day that the New York Times printed a comprehensive story about Dr. Rost's whistle-blowing role at his former employer. Thus, a jury could reasonably draw an inference that Pfizer shied away from hiring a documented whistle-blower for one particular senior position, knowing full well of his protected activity the previous November.

Jon also stated in the letter that I did want to work:

Dr. Rost is desirous of resolving his issues with Pfizer amicably by taking on a position with Pfizer commensurate with his abilities. Therefore, Dr. Rost, through this office, is requesting a tolling agreement for an indefinite period so that discussions may take place in an atmosphere conducive to resolution.

Since I stood a poor chance of landing another pharma-industry job, I was more than willing to work for Pfizer in a real job, so long as they treated me fairly and dealt squarely with the legal issues I had raised. I didn't want my professional skills to wither.

Pfizer Signs an Agreement

The letter to Pfizer led to something that is called a "tolling agreement,"[5] which meant that if I did sue Pfizer, or vice versa, we didn't have to worry about statutes of limitations, which, for many laws, were only one year.

So I could take legal action at a later time and didn't need to move forward right away. The benefit to both parties was that it gave us time to resolve our differences without going to court.

The one thing the agreement didn't do, though, was resolve *my* situation. And I was starting to get really, really bored. It was April of 2004; the first anniversary of Pfizer's take-over had come and gone. I had to come up with something to do—I just didn't know what.

FIFTEEN

An Explosive Book Review

IN LIFE, THERE ARE CERTAIN SMALL EVENTS that we don't recognize immediately but that have the potential to change our future forever. I was about to encounter one of those situations. As the summer of 2004 drew to an end, I grew more and more frustrated about my position. To be paid well to do nothing may sound like a dream come true; however, it was paired with a nagging uncertainty about my future.

After signing the tolling agreement, Pfizer refused to further discuss my situation with me or my lawyer. The only small ray of hope came in the summer of 2004, when Pfizer's lawyers asked us for an estimate of the damages we thought we'd be able to prove in court. We responded to their request. Since it didn't look as if I would get another job, and I was paid well, the damages we thought we could prove was large—over $10 million. We never received a formal response from Pfizer and silence settled again. Clearly they wanted to keep us guessing about what would happen next.

I felt as though I were being held hostage. I couldn't flee, since my most important reference refused to return calls from prospective employers. On top of it all, I had always been a very hardworking individual who loved to deliver results. This forced idleness was not something I enjoyed. But I also knew that this was part of the battle: to make me sweat so that I would break down. That was the last thing I would permit myself to do.

And then something interesting happened. I came across Marcia Angell's book, *The Truth about the Drug Companies*. Reading that book would change a lot for me. Angell had written a terrific exposé that described, in detail, how the drug companies operate and how they market drugs. I recognized all the practices she described and realized that, to an outsider, it might not sound very ethical, although to someone in the industry this was simply how things were done.

I had always had a dream of one day running a pharmaceutical company and changing the business for the better. I wanted to make money but also make a difference, both for employees and patients. In a small way I had been able to do this when I was working overseas and lowered drug prices. Then it hit me—I didn't really have anything holding me back from speaking the truth already today. Perhaps the fact that I was now a vice president at a major pharmaceutical company would give me the credibility to step forward; perhaps I didn't have to wait for a more senior position that might never materialize. I decided to dip my toe in the water. I figured if this was my destiny, if this was meant to be, then a short book review on amazon.com might lead to an avalanche. It was almost like rolling the dice, only now I gambled my career and the future of my family, to make a difference. This is what I wrote about Angell's book:

***** **FANTASTIC READING**, August 25, 2004

I should start with a disclaimer. I'm a Vice President within one of the largest drug companies in the world and I have spent close to twenty years marketing drugs. So I guess I'm not supposed to like this book. But the truth is I thought it was fantastic.

First, for those of you who are not familiar with the healthcare industry, you should know that Ms. Angell is better capable of writing this masterpiece than any other author. She used to be Editor-in-Chief of the New England Journal of Medicine, which is considered the most prestigious medical journal in the world. Don't let her credentials scare you off, though. This is easy reading and the book captures your attention like a true business thriller, only this is real life suspense.

But this volume is much more than simple entertainment. It is quite possibly one of the best analyses of the state of the U.S. drug industry today, complete with footnotes backing up every statement the author makes. You will learn not only that in 2002 the top ten drug companies made a higher profit than the other 490 businesses together on the Fortune 500 list. You will also understand how the drug industry has been able to achieve such a business success and how this success, as is often the case throughout history, will likely be their downfall.

A political tidal wave is building which will forever change both the industry and many of its infamous business practices. It is sad to note that the drug industry today is as equally poorly regarded as the tobacco companies, and this is a testament not only to the shortsighted foolishness of their management, but also to the fact that you can fool some of the customers some of the time, but not all of them all the time.

So is there no hope? Well, Ms. Angell doesn't only state the problem, she also presents solutions and ends her story with several thoughtful suggestions on how to change the way we discover, market and distribute new drugs. Her advice is wise and absent of quick fixes. Only time will tell if there will be a movement so strong that it can defeat ingrained business practices of the richest companies in the world.

What may help is that the drug companies are their own worst enemies. They have antagonized grannies all over the U.S. with their work to stop reimportation of cheaper drugs into the U.S., a practice that has been in place for many years in Europe. And anyone in marketing or public relations can tell you that no money in the world can help you win against millions of mad grandmothers.

Only a few days later Rita Rubin from *USA Today* contacted me. Rita penned an article and stated, "Surprisingly, Peter Rost, a vice president at drug giant Pfizer, sides with Angell. He posted a 5-star review of her book on Amazon.com." Then she quoted me saying that "It's really hard to find new drugs, and it's getting harder and harder. There is a lot of low-hanging fruit out there that has been picked off. It is very, very difficult to really find a breakthrough."[1] I also told her that drugmakers "focus on tweaking existing drugs to make money, not to advance science."

A Decision That Would Change Everything

The call from Rita Rubin served as an indicator that perhaps speaking up about the drug industry was indeed my destiny. I had spent almost twenty years working in the pharmaceutical sector; I had delivered high-performance results, and I knew the European market well and how reimportation of drugs had been done safely and cost-effectively in Europe for over twenty years. Still, in the U.S., the drug industry claimed Americans couldn't handle this process. I knew the industry wasn't honest in their arguments against drug importation. So I decided the *USA Today* article was the sign I needed to go on the offense, even though the consequences were unforeseeable. I already had a history of speaking out, trying to do the right thing internally, so speaking out publicly was just a matter of applying what I had done quietly in my job—be straightforward and honest with my arguments. Finally I would do something productive again. Now it was just a matter of finding an audience.

The first thing I did was to contact the former mayor of Springfield, Massachusetts, Michael Albano. I had read about how he had helped push through a measure to allow 9,000 Springfield employees and retirees to purchase Canadian prescription drugs. I left a message with him and it didn't take long for him to return my call. But he didn't just call me, he had a proposal.

"I'm going to speak at the annual meeting of the Society for Professional Journalists on Friday. It's in New York and I'd like to share half of my time with you," he said.

It was already Monday so I had to make up my mind immediately. Suddenly, I wasn't just dipping my toe in the water. I had to decide if I was going to swim with the sharks. This was not a difficult decision. I don't agonize over decisions; on the contrary, my challenge is to restrain myself from not making them too fast. I have learned that it is a good thing to sleep for a night before venturing ahead with things that can have a major impact on others or me. I did talk to my wife about this opportunity, and she wasn't entirely enthusiastic about the prospect of me speaking out publicly on the issue of reimportation of drugs. But sometimes a goal feels so right; you just know you have to do it. My wife reluctantly agreed that this was one of those situations.

I didn't know if Pfizer would use this as an excuse to fire me, since I took a different position than the one the company had officially sanctioned, or if my legal case against them would somehow crumble. Still, I left the house on that Friday morning ready to speak my mind to hundreds of journalists gathered at the meeting in New York. My heart was pounding and I felt reinvigorated. I couldn't wait to get up on the podium. This would be my first step to expose the falsehoods the pharmaceutical industry had told the public.

When I arrived in the conference room, I was sorely disappointed. It turned out that this was a satellite symposium and less than half a dozen journalists had found this particular event. Still, I spoke out. I told those listening how drug reimportation had become a success story in Europe. I argued that the free market would prevail, and that drug makers would thrive, ultimately, in a competitive arena.

The following day David Schwab wrote in the New Jersey *Star-Ledger*, "It's not every day a successful executive embarks on a personal campaign criticizing the very industry in which he has worked for over 20 years—especially the pharmaceutical industry. But that's where Peter Rost found himself yesterday as he addressed a gathering of journalists in New York and strongly criticized the effort by drug makers to prevent the importing of cheaper medicines from overseas."[2]

In her Associated Press article, Theresa Agovino echoed this sentiment: "Importing inexpensive prescription drugs has a new and unlikely ally: a Pfizer Inc. executive." Then she quoted me, "We have to speak out for the people who can't afford drugs, in favor of free trade and against a closed market."[3]

The Washington Post Makes a Difference

The same day, Michael Albano suggested that I come with him to Montgomery County, Maryland, where the FDA is located, to do a press conference the following Monday. There, television cameras waited and so did a much larger number of reporters.

The biggest newspaper to cover the event was the *Washington Post*. It ended its article with a quote from me, "I think it is derogatory to suggest Americans would not be able to handle the reimportation of drugs when the rest of the educated world can do this." The *Washington Post* also quoted me saying, "I think the industry looks at this in the same way the National Rifle Association looks at gun control. They are afraid if there is a crack in the wall, the whole dam will come bursting."[4]

On my way back home from the press conference, National Public Radio called me and asked for an instant interview, which I did—parked beside the road. The next day the *Washington Post* landed in front of the lawmakers on Capitol Hill.

SIXTEEN

Risking Everything

THE *WASHINGTON POST* ARTICLE CAUGHT THE NOTICE of several lawmakers in the U.S. Congress. Within a day, I received a call from the office of Congressman Bernie Sanders (I-VT). His aide told me that a bipartisan group of senators and members of Congress wanted me to come to Washington to participate in a panel to discuss reimportation of drugs. On September 20, I received the official fax from Senator Byron Dorgan and nine members of Congress: Bernard Sanders, Jo Ann Emerson, Sherrod Brown, Gil Gutknecht, Rahm Emanuel, Dan Burton, Rosa DeLauro, Marion Berry, and James Langevin.

For me, a regular guy who had never been involved in politics, much less ever met a congressman or senator, it was an honor to receive that letter, signed by every one of them and with the "Congress of United States" seal on the letterhead. I marveled at it, reading it over and over again. Only about ten years earlier, I hadn't even been a U.S. citizen, and now some of the key decision makers from the most powerful legislative body in the world wanted me to help them. I felt humbled.

On this official stationery I was told that, ". . . we will host a panel discussion on the issue of prescription drug importation and the legislative proposals now pending before Congress. We are trying to create a balanced panel that can present all points of view on this issue."

Others invited included Alan Holmer, President and CEO of PhRMA, the industry organization for pharmaceutical companies, and Marcia Angell, who had written the book *The Truth About the Drug Companies*, as well as Chistopher Viehbacher, President of the U.S. division of GlaxoSmithKline.

It didn't take long until both PhRMA and GlaxoSmithKline had declined to participate. Equipped with poor arguments, this was a no win situation for them. No one could locate Dr. Angell. So that left me alone.

Kicked Out of CNBC's Waiting Room

While preparation for the DC press conference took place, I was getting more attention from the press. For the first time in my life, television stations started calling. The first call was from Bianna Golodryga, producer for CNBC. She said that Maria Bartiromo wanted to interview me for about ten minutes the following day.

One way PR agencies make money is to "media train" employees of major corporations. Usually, this entails being placed in front of a camera with a retired journalist shooting questions at you in rapid succession. I had gone through three of these training sessions, but I had never had any use for them, until now. The reality is that very few corporate employees ever see a real television camera.

On the day when I was going to be interviewed, CNBC sent a limousine to pick me up and take me to their headquarters in Secaucus, New Jersey. When we arrived I noticed that several other Lincoln Town cars also waited outside the headquarters. The grey building looked like any huge warehouse; inside the lobby was sparsely furnished. I was whisked away to a waiting room. After a while, it was time for my makeup. A friendly woman with a white coat and a spray bottle in her hand greeted me. I sat down in an old-fashioned barber chair and stared into a wall of mirrors with lights around them. The lady did my hair, then proceeded to pick up something that resembled a spray-paint can. It turned out that it *was* spray paint, to be used for my face. It produced a nice, brown tan. When my hair and makeup were done, she escorted me back to the waiting room.

But now I wasn't alone in the waiting room. Three extremely tall guys with shaved heads, crisp suits, and gold watches had gathered there. I had no idea who they were; they looked like very large basketball players. The first thing they did was look at me, smile, then politely say that they were discussing something private and wondered if I would mind waiting in the corridor. I looked them over, saw bulging muscles under serious faces, and nodded in agreement, although I felt it was a pretty arrogant request.

After another ten minutes, I was taken into the studio. It was the size of a football field, with rows upon rows of computerized workstations, and then in the second half of the vast expanse, there were sets for various shows on small risers with television cameras surrounding them. Bright lights with multicolored filters lit up the room; the whole place looked spectacular.

My First Live Interview

I was taken straight to Maria Bartiromo and Mike Huckman. Maria greeted me warmly and we sat down at a large, glass table with several cameras trained on us. I was told we were going to be on air in only a couple of minutes, and then the show started. When the lights came on was when I got really nervous, but I forgot all about that as soon as Maria and Mike started to pepper me with hard-hitting questions. I barely had a chance to think—lucky thing that I am such an opinionated guy.

My first lesson from that interview was that I should have smiled more: Smiles work great on camera. My second lesson was that if I hadn't known my stuff, I would have been in serious trouble. Maria and Mike were very well-prepared. Another thing I learned (probably taught in Politics 101) was that if I didn't feel as if a question took the discussion in the right direction, I could answer whatever I wanted.

They didn't have the time or inclination to go back and insist on a particular answer. My dimly-remembered media training had paid off, but perhaps not in the way the companies that provided it had expected.

When we were done, Maria grabbed my hand, looked into my eyes and said, "That was really great, Peter. It's amazing that you're doing this." I don't know if she agreed with my position, but she certainly gave me the impression that she admired that fact that I stuck my neck out.

As I walked out, I passed by another podium with Jim Cramer and Larry Kudlow, of the *Kudlow & Cramer* show. They were preparing to go on air, but Larry couldn't resist giving me a disapproving glare. He shouted at me, "You're ruining everything. How can you do this?"

"You don't agree with me?" I stopped and asked with a smile.

He waved me away dismissively.

"Listen, if you'd like to, I'd be happy to come on your show and debate this with you . . ." We were interrupted by a producer who said we had to stop talking, because the show was about to go live.

More Calls from Television Stations

The following day, I had two television interviews in New York: One with Neil Cavuto on Fox News and another for the Canadian Broadcast Corporation. Just as with CNBC, I was picked up by a car and whisked off to my appearances. While I was waiting outside the Fox studio, I got another re-touch by the make-up people, and then I had a chance to meet some of the guests who were going on before me.

One of the guests was a money manager, and when he heard I worked for Pfizer his face lit up. He told me he loved that company and that he held a ton of Pfizer stock. Later on he said the same thing on television. I didn't say much. As a company employee, I avoided saying anything whatsoever about Pfizer. But I couldn't resist thinking what a sucker he was. I had cashed in my stock options earlier in the year when the stock peaked. The stock had since then dropped; however, every newsletter in the country still recommended Pfizer stock, in spite of the recent loss in value. A few months later, that big money manager must have lost a fortune, because the stock dropped another 25 percent.

I figured that Fox, being a pretty conservative channel, would come down hard on me. I was mistaken. Neil Cavuto was tough but compassionate in his questioning, and he appeared genuinely sympathetic. After the television cameras were turned off, he pulled me aside and wanted to know the inside story that I had refused to tell him on camera. What was going on when I went to work, what my bosses had said, and that sort of thing. I knew that one is never really off record with any journalist, so I didn't tell him anything more. This I feel bad about now, since I liked him and he appeared genuinely trustworthy. I later learned that you *can* tell journalists things off the record if you have an ongoing relationship with them and mutual respect. It is no different than asking a friend to keep a secret. Some you can trust, some you can't.

My Concerned Lawyer

I have to admit that my lawyer was not happy about all this. His job was to protect my legal case, which he told me was excellent. The fact that I was speaking up made me vulnerable and could have ruined the whole case. He was surely right that I took a big risk, but I felt that it was more important that I got the message out. And after a few months, Jon even said that I was doing a pretty good job. "Who knows," he admitted. "You might actually achieve some change."

Pfizer was taken completely by surprise by my media blitz, and it took them about a week to hire a law firm to handle this new situation. Pfizer had a policy which stated that "employees are not authorized to answer questions from the news media." This was why I avoided making any comments about Pfizer's business and also requested that journalists and television anchors state that I spoke as a private citizen, and not as a Pfizer employee.

Many newspapers were surprised that I hadn't been fired outright. They didn't know that Pfizer had already illegally threatened to terminate me, so the laws that could be used against them under this act still applied. What made matters worse for Pfizer was that my lawyer had asked for my reinstatement without any particular conditions, and said I wanted to continue to work, and they had refused to give me something meaningful to do. It is also important to remember that most states have laws making it illegal for companies to fire workers who participate in legally permissible political activities. Those activities may be protected if they occur on the employee's own time, off company premises, and without the use of employer property or equipment. So an employee's off-the-job political activities are off limits to his or her employer. Federal law also prohibits discrimination on the basis of political affiliation. But journalists and news anchors were still very surprised that I didn't get fired. It was as if everyone had forgotten that we live in a democracy with freedom of speech and other basic rights.

Pfizer could have chosen to fire me regardless—and take the fight when I filed a civil suit, but they chose not to do that. There *was* something Pfizer might have been really nervous about. Two weeks prior to my invitation to Capitol Hill, I informed Pfizer that I had provided truthful information to the FBI, the FDA's Enforcement Division and the New York State Attorney's office, based on internal Pfizer documents. Now, if they did something to me they might violate U.S. criminal law, which provides that "anyone who interferes with the lawful employment or livelihood of a person, for providing to a law enforcement officer any truthful information relating to the commission or possible commission of any Federal offense, may be imprisoned up to 10 years."

SEVENTEEN

Fanning the Flames on Capitol Hill

WHEN THE MEDIA FOUND OUT that I was going to Capitol Hill to do a press conference with a number of congressmen and senators, they went into overdrive. Now this wasn't just a story of a vice president who spoke his mind; it was national news about a single pharma executive standing up to the entire industry.

New Jersey's *Star-Ledger* hired a photographer to come to my home and take pictures; later, the *Boston Globe* did the same. The funny thing was that they both ended up hiring the same A.P. photographer, so he laughed when, on the second day, he returned to do, essentially, the same job. Dozens of newspapers interviewed me over several days, even from as far away as Canada and Sweden. I could hardly put down the receiver before the phone rang again. CNBC wanted to do another segment, so Maria Bartiromo invited me to tape an op-ed for her *Wall Street Journal Report* while I was in Washington. Scott Hensley wrote in the *Wall Street Journal,* "In speaking out against his employer's position on a public issue, Dr. Rost walks a thin line. There are few protections for employees in the private sector to speak out as he has."[1] When Scott spoke with me, he was completely incredulous that I still had my job at Pfizer. He said, "If I ever did something like that to the *Wall Street Journal,* they'd have me out the door right away. How come Pfizer doesn't fire you?"

Of course, I couldn't answer his question.

Pfizer's Counter Attack

A week before my press conference on Capitol Hill, on September 16, 2004, my attorney received a letter from Clark Finkelberg of Colman, Zimmer & Krasnoff. This is a 170-year-old law firm with more than 900 lawyers in eighteen offices around the world. Apparently employees like that firm, because a major law journal had highlighted Colman, Zimmer & Krasnoff as one of the "Best 50 Firms to Work For."

I didn't know what Pfizer's objective was and why they had hired a new law firm to investigate me, although I soon discovered that Colman, Zimmer & Krasnoff had represented corporate plaintiffs in a lawsuit against two former employees in a highly-publicized defamation lawsuit. Colman, Zimmer & Krasnoff won that suit; however, the California Supreme Court set aside the jury's verdict that had required the two former workers to pay almost a million dollars for posting defamatory remarks about company executives. Justice Judd Black wrote for the 6-1 court, "You have a right not to be dragged through the courts because you exercised your constitutional rights."

In his letter, Mr. Finkelberg said that his firm had been retained the day prior to interrogate me about my statements regarding importation of prescription drugs. The letter also emphasized that Finkelberg had been retained solely to investigate this area and no other issue that may or may not relate to my employment. It also said that I, as a Pfizer employee, was obligated to participate in the inquiry.

What One Lawyer Didn't Want to Know

Mr. Finkelberg's first interrogation took place on September 21, 2004, one day ahead of my Washington press conference, in Jon Green's office. Right before the meeting was about to start, Jon received a phone call from the lawyers at Partland & Longhorn. They were, apparently, very upset and told him that if I didn't stop talking to the press, Pfizer wouldn't continue their discussions about a settlement with me. Jon spoke to me, and I told him to "forget about it." I couldn't care less what Pfizer's lawyers were threatening us with and their screams on the phone were pathetic. I wasn't going to be blackmailed by them. I stood next to Jon when he responded, "Whaddaya mean? They haven't even *started* talking to him." It couldn't have been said more succinctly. In fact, Pfizer had refused to discuss anything related to my employment situation after Jon sent the letter with my estimated damages. I could tell from Jon's chuckle when he hung up that he enjoyed the situation.

Back in the conference room, Mr. Finkelberg started off by telling me that I had no right to have an attorney present in an internal Pfizer investigation, and that Pfizer had agreed to Mr. Green's presence as a courtesy. I felt very thankful that my employer was so considerate, but I also realized that if they had decided to shake me up in private, it might not have looked good in this kind of high-profile situation.

Mr. Finkelberg also emphasized that he didn't want to know anything about any other legal matters that Pfizer and I were discussing. He kept emphasizing this point over and over again, since he might not have been able to question me if he knew of my recent letter to Ronald Chapman and Hank McKinnell stating that I was a witness in an ongoing criminal investigation against Pfizer, and that I had given information to various law enforcement officers related to the possible commission of federal offenses.

Mr. Finkelberg started his questioning by informing me that he was aware of my upcoming proceeding before Congress. He then asked for details about this particular event and why newspapers had started to write about me. The meeting was relatively cordial and gave me the opportunity to explain to him the "four legal pillars" that gave me the right to speak out publicly without expecting retaliation. I told him that I had spoken out publicly about Wyeth a year earlier without any reprimand from Pharmacia, that I had informed Pfizer about the articles dealing with the Wyeth litigation without their objection, and that I followed Pfizer business policy on press contacts by establishing that I spoke as a private citizen. Finally, I reminded him that there were laws that protected free speech and political activity. Mr. Finkelberg filled page after page of yellow pads with notes, then dismissed me.

An Illegal Request?

The next day, on September 22, 2004, Mr. Finkelberg sent a second letter to Jon. The letter said that "Since your client told us that he plans to continue . . . his public appearances, we . . . insist that Mr. Rost provide the Company with sufficient advance notice . . . before meeting with public officials, so that the Company has an opportunity to respond appropriately, including by correcting his uninformed statements."

There was a significant problem with this request, since it disclosed that Pfizer had the intention of interfering with any contacts I may have planned with elected representatives, including Congress. It could be argued that this request attempted to dissuade me from attending the scheduled proceeding before Congress, as well as any future proceedings before Congress, and this could make it a violation of certain criminal laws. §1512 in the U.S. criminal code states that "Whoever intentionally harasses another person and thereby hinders, delays, prevents, or dissuades any person from attending or testifying in an official proceeding; shall be fined under this title or imprisoned not more than one year, or both."[2] According to another paragraph, the term "official proceeding" is defined as a "proceeding before the Congress."[3]

The Press Conference

The next day, on the morning of the press conference, the first thing I did was to check the news, using my laptop. Congressman Emanual Rahm (D-IL) had released a statement saying, "I would like to nominate Dr. Rost for the Guts of the Year award. Courageous whistleblowers like Dr. Rost have helped make the tobacco industry accountable for misconceptions about the health risks of smoking."[4] He added, "I want to thank Dr. Rost for blowing the whistle on the pharmaceutical industry, breaking down myths perpetuated by the industry that help keep prices—and profits—high at the expense of American families."

David Schwab at the *Star-Ledger* expressed what was on many minds. "Most people probably find it hard to fathom why Peter Rost would want to stir up the pharmaceutical industry in such dramatic—and possibly risky—fashion. Rost, an executive at drug maker Pfizer, concedes many might think him nuts for mounting a personal crusade—on his own time—challenging the powerful and secretive drug makers on one of the most controversial issues: the high price of prescription medicines." David continued, "The decision to speak out is just the latest unconventional move for Rost, who has worked as a fashion model, earned a medical degree, written books on surgery and used cars, started a medical advertising agency and, after a successful run at drug maker Wyeth, got demoted for exposing what he contended in a lawsuit was a tax fraud." David then quoted me saying, "I have consistently tried to make the impossible happen. I realize that to a lot of people this sounds nuts. But you know what? Everything I have succeeded in doing in the past sounded nuts."[5]

David was suspicious about my situation and he did everything from checking that I still had an office at Pfizer to trying out my phone and fax numbers on my business cards. In short, David did everything a good journalist should do. But only I knew the full scope of my situation; that I was sitting on a legal time bomb that could explode at any time.

Capitol Hill

After an exquisite breakfast at the hotel, I took a cab to one of the congressional office buildings for the big meeting. There were big, white, imposing buildings all around me with metal detectors and long lines outside the entrances. In fact, all of Capitol Hill looked like we were at war, with police officers wearing boots and machine guns at every corner and big boulders blocking would-be terrorists. Inside I could tell that this had been real fancy quarters fifty years ago with stone and marble all over the place, but it was equally clear that time had left its patina, and not much renovation had taken place, giving these powerful government buildings a run-down and shoddy appearance.

In my initial meeting with Congressman Sanders and his staff, who had planned the event, they were very careful to point out that this was a bipartisan issue and that I shouldn't take any political position in favor of Republicans or Democrats. That wasn't hard advice to follow, since I considered myself an independent.

After a cup of coffee in a paper mug in the large cafeteria with fake wood tables and spindly chairs, we left for the Dirksen Senate Office building. This was a nicer building with elaborate decorations. Congressman Sanders had given me a heads-up that the press interest was significant, but I couldn't have imagined how large. As we approached the room where the press conference was going to be held, journalists and television cameras swarmed around me.

Pfizer Shoots Themselves in the Foot

As ten o'clock approached, congressional staff had to cut my comments short to reporters and television cameras outside, and they led me into the meeting room. It was a large room, completely wood paneled, jam-packed with journalists and about fifteen television cameras. Behind the speaker's chair, around eight or nine congressmen and senators had gathered.

As we started the press conference, there was a big surprise waiting for me. Pfizer had sent a letter to each participant, in which they stated that, "We understand that you have invited Dr. Peter Rost to join in a press conference and panel discussion on drug importation on September 23. Dr. Rost has no qualifications to speak on importation, no responsibilities in this area at Pfizer, no knowledge of the information and analysis Pfizer has provided to the government on this issue, and no substantive grasp of how importation may impact the safety of this nation's drug supply."

The letter immediately backfired. Senator Byron Dorgan (D-ND), in his introductory speech, held up the letter and declared tongue-in-cheek that he didn't feel it was credible, because it had misspelled his name, and Representative Anne M. Northup, (R-KY), said, "The letter was insulting. It regurgitated the same sort of claims they have made in the past, claims that have been refuted."[6]

The congressmen continued to make many sharp comments about the drug industry. Senator Dorgan, chief sponsor of the reimportation bill in the Senate, said, "Miracle drugs offer no miracles for people who cannot take them because of the cost."[7] Senator Olympia Snowe (R-ME) added, "If European countries can safely trade prescription drugs, the United States should be up to the task as well,"[8] while Representative Marion Berry (D-AR) emphasized, "Here we are in a global economy, and the United States allows these drug companies to take advantage and rob our own people. That can't continue."[9]

When the elected representatives were done presenting their views, they had yet another surprise for me. Because of Pfizer's letter, Representative Jo Ann Emerson (R-MO), gave me a military flak jacket.

"You might want to take this back to Pfizer," she said and the ensuing photo-op when she handed over the camouflage jacket, made the room light up with photo flashes. The seasoned members of Congress had taken Pfizer's letter and turned it around to one of the best moments of the press conference. And now it was my turn to speak.

The Most Important Speech of my Life

I looked out over the packed room, glanced at both my sides where the congressmen and senators surrounded me and then eyed my notes. My heart didn't race, but I felt the tension build inside as my stomach tied into a knot. I knew the only route forward was to dive right in.

But I stopped myself for a few seconds. I also knew that for the speaker, time goes about ten times faster than it does for the audience. That is what all that adrenaline does for you, which is part of your body's "fight or flight" reaction. You are ready to run, to react rapidly to defend yourself. Only, when you speak publicly you don't have anyone to defend yourself against; your worst enemy is actually you and the fact that you lose the sense of time. So knowing that, I looked back up again, over the audience.

I waited for a moment that felt like an eternity but probably only lasted a few seconds. The room became absolutely silent, and then I started.

I told the cameras that "the most important healthcare issue today is reimportation. We have 67 million Americans without insurance for drugs. They pay cash, full price. And many of them don't get the drugs they need, because they cannot afford our high prices."

Then I went straight for the jugular of those who oppose drug importation. "The biggest argument against reimportation is safety. What everyone has conveniently forgotten to tell you is that in Europe, reimportation of drugs has been in place for twenty years."

This was my key message. If everyone lost interest after this introduction, they would still remember that other countries could do it, and had done it for decades. This fact, alone, obliterated all of Big Pharma's arguments against drug importation.

Once I got into the stride of my speech it wasn't hard—I was determined to make people hear my message. To really drive home that point I said, "During my time responsible for a region in northern

Europe, I never once—*not once*—heard the drug industry, regulatory agencies, the government, or anyone else saying that this practice was unsafe. And, personally, I think it is outright derogatory to claim that Americans would not be able to handle reimportation of drugs, when the rest of the educated world can do this." Appealing to America's sense of pride as a nation was crucial, in order to put misinformation from the drug industry into perspective. It worked. This became one of the most repeated quotes from my presentation.

Now it was time to put the lack of affordable drugs into perspective. "So why is reimportation important? It is important because reimportation has a major impact on drug prices and a lot of people can't afford life-saving drugs today. They don't take them, the drugs don't work. When drugs don't work, people die." Then I said, "I believe we have to speak out for the people who can't afford drugs, in favor of free trade and against a closed market."

The WHO has the numbers that prove our failure: Americans have shorter life expectancies, higher infant-mortality rates, and higher child-mortality rates than virtually all countries in Western Europe.

I added, "But let me comfort you: We did beat them all in one area! Our healthcare costs are twice as high as theirs. And our costs for individual drugs are sometimes twice as high, even ten times as high. The difference, between them and us, is that they all have affordable drugs."

It was time to lighten the somber mood that started to settle over the room: "Are we fools, unable to stop this madness? Abraham Lincoln said 'You can fool some of the people some of the time but not all of them all the time.' And Abraham Lincoln hadn't even read the February 2004 issue of *Pharmaceutical Executive*."

As I had hoped, the audience started laughing. "Let me tell you what they say," I said. "One of the most dangerous trends in public opinion is the big increase in those who know that drugs cost much more in the United States than they do in other countries." Just in case anyone would have missed the take-home point, I said, "So to know is a dangerous trend, according to Pharma's key magazine."

At this point in the speech, it was time to reinforce what made my talk really powerful; the fact that I was an industry executive. I stated, "The article goes on to say that 'Only 13 percent believe the drug industry is generally honest and trustworthy.' Can you imagine how I feel as a drug executive about this? Nine out of ten Americans don't think big pharma is honest and trustworthy."

Before my presentation, I had been advised by some of the congressmen that they all still remembered when the tobacco executives had been on the Hill and had claimed that smoking was safe. They bristled at this recollection and this had given me an idea for what to say and how to connect the way Big Pharma behaved today with how the tobacco companies had tried to fool the American public many years earlier.

"What other business with such a rating could even hope to survive? If you think of the tobacco companies, you're right. As a matter of fact, the reputation of the pharma industry today, an industry that saves lives, is now approaching the tobacco industry; an industry that saves very few lives, an industry that ten years ago testified in congress that smoking was safe. Today the drug industry testifies that reimportation is not safe."

There was something else that was important for me to communicate: That I wasn't an opponent of the drug industry. This was an industry I really liked, and I didn't just think they were wrong on this issue; I also thought they were hurting themselves, long-term. "One of the things I've learned in business is that if you don't change what you do, you will not get different results. And it is time for pharma to change what they do. And would it really be so bad? I don't think so. Let me tell you a story from actually living with reimportation.

"When I was overseas and started to lose a lot of sales to my colleagues in southern Europe, I responded by lowering some of my own prices. The result was that in an area in which one of my drugs competed with the biggest drug in the world, sold by AstraZeneca, in their home market, we went from a 5 percent to 30 percent market share in 18 months. So the free market rewarded us. You see, I do care about company profits. I've spent my life creating those profits. I don't only speak out to help patients, but also to wake up the drug companies, because they are certainly not helping themselves right now."

And there was something more going on; something Big Pharma had been good at hiding. Now was the time to say it, so that the American people would understand the game going on with their money: "And perhaps, all of this wouldn't be so bad if we helped truly needy American corporations; corporations that laid the golden egg. But that is not the case. Half the large drug companies are foreign corporations. Why should we allow them to come in and gouge our American tax payers?"

I had one final example to give, an example that would show that Big Pharma's arguments that lower prices would hurt R&D simply didn't hold water and I used Merck as an example. "In 2003, Merck recorded revenue of $22.5 billion. Of this, they spent $3.2 billion on R&D. That's not quite as much as they paid out in dividends—$3.3 billion, and much, much less than their 'marketing, sales and administrative' costs—$6.4 billion. After other charges and taxes, the company still recorded profit of $6.8 billion."

The Media Tells the Story

After I had spoken, half a dozen of reporters gathered around me with recorders and notepads in their hands. The day continued with photo shoots in the afternoon and additional interviews. The sun was shining; the weather was beautiful; and the Capitol Hill backdrop couldn't have been presented more favorably. It was an amazing experience for someone who had never been in the public eye in the past.

The following day, articles in newspapers and reports on television indicated that my message had hit a homerun. The *New York Times* summarized my comments in an article that started, "A dissident executive from Pfizer, the world's largest drug maker, denounced the pharmaceutical industry on Thursday for resisting legislation that would allow imports of low-cost prescription drugs from Canada and other countries." The *Times* wrote that my comments gave new life to a failing effort to pass such legislation. Then they quoted me saying, "Holding up a vote on importation, stopping good importation bills has a high, high cost not just in money, but in American lives. Every day we delay, Americans die because they cannot afford life-saving drugs."[10]

The *Times* had also talked to a Pfizer spokesperson, who told the newspaper that Pfizer had not tried to silence me, however, he expressed irritation: "His comments impugn the integrity of employees at Pfizer and other companies that have cited the risks of imported drugs."

Pfizer also was quoted stating that, "Peter Rost continues to maintain that he is speaking for himself at the same time that he is clearly identifying himself as a Pfizer employee. In doing so, this represents a clear conflict . . . And we find his comments derogatory and misleading."[11]

The funniest comment was printed by the Wilmington *Star*:

> Pfizer is peeved with Dr. Peter Rost, of course. It issued a statement saying, in effect, that he doesn't know what he's talking about. One thing he's talking about is that some Americans can't afford the wonderful drugs Pfizer and other companies make, and as a result, some Americans are dying.
>
> That would seem to be factual.
>
> Another thing he's talking about is that European countries have long allowed prescription drugs to be exported and imported, and Europeans by the score aren't keeling over from bad medicine.
>
> That would seem to be factual.
>
> Here's another fact: Even the pro-business U.S. House of Representatives has passed a bill that would legalize drug imports, and the U.S. Senate probably would follow suit except for one thing. Or rather, one person: Bill Frist, the Republican majority leader. He won't let it come to a vote. As

his spokesman explained, 'Until he sees a way we can do this safely, he won't put the American people in jeopardy.' Apparently Sen. Frist doesn't think the American people are in jeopardy because they can't afford to buy prescription drugs.[12]

Soon the editorial pages of heartland America were filled with headlines, such as the one in Chattanooga *Times Free Press*, saying, "Dr. Frist, tear down this death wall!"[13]

EIGHTEEN

A Political Inquisition

IT DIDN'T TAKE LONG AFTER I SPOKE OUT ON CAPITOL HILL for my e-mail inbox to fill with notes from Pfizer colleagues, most of whom I had never met or heard of before. It wasn't just rank and file employees who contacted me—I also received mail from colleagues who worked in Pfizer's government-relations department, and they clearly weren't happy about my performance. Their comments made it sound as if I were a sinner who needed to be brought back to the path of the righteous.

The biggest surprise, however, wasn't the flood of e-mails, or that many employees were upset about what I had said. The biggest surprise was that so many actually agreed with my comments. In fact, about 40 percent of the e-mails I received were supportive. I imagine it took a lot more guts to write a positive e-mail than to send a critical message and copy a superior. In truth, I wished my supporters hadn't written, since I assumed that Pfizer was reading my e-mail. The following is a typical comment from someone who was upset by my comments about reimportation of drugs: "You must be extremely disgruntled to do something like this. Why even work at Pfizer if you can't support the Company, much less the entire industry? It's a shame to have employees like you who add fuel to the fire, feeding the ignorance of the American public."

Another one wrote, "The ethical thing would be to resign and then make your attack. I am sorry but as far as I am concerned you don't have much credibility if you continue to behave in the way you are doing at present. If you believe Pfizer and other pharmaceutical companies are acting in an unethical manner, how can you in good conscience work for one? I leave you with that thought."

One writer believed in free speech, but not in me. "While I support your right to speak (I saw you on Fox News today), I have to tell you. I think you are an angry, misguided individual."

Another point of view was held by a director from a competing drug company—in the corporate communications department, of all places. He wrote, "As a pharmaceutical industry employee myself who holds similar views, I can only hope that your faith that 'Pfizer is an equal-opportunity employer' that accommodates a 'diversity of opinions,' is justified. I doubt it, though, and wish you luck."

But there were also many people who wrote simple messages of support, such as, "Thank you for integrity, guts and honesty. You do have a team behind you," or, "Good for you for speaking out on an important and personally costly issue. I admire your integrity and courage."

Even a retiree wrote and agreed with me, "I applaud your efforts to encourage a more constructive approach to pharmaceutical importation. As a recent retiree from Pfizer, I am worried that by being short-sighted, Pfizer is doing something that is not its own best interest."

This was exactly my point of view. I wasn't *against* the drug industry. I liked this industry and appreciated the things that these companies do for humankind. But I was against their shortsighted focus on profit at the expense of human suffering. I believed their focus on increasing the value of their stock options would cost the industry much more than they gained during the few years that they would manage to prevent reimportation. About the only people I *didn't* hear from were my direct supervisors, which perhaps wasn't very surprising since they had stayed away from me ever since I started reporting to them. In fact, I hadn't heard a word from either one of my two bosses during the past year.

The Interrogation

When I returned from Washington, it was time for another meeting with Colman, Zimmer & Krasnoff. On September 29, I had to go to Jon's office to meet Mr. Finkelberg again. This time the questioning was a lot more hostile, and shortly into the meeting Jon advised me that it would be in my best interest to have the meeting recorded. Initially, Mr. Finkelberg refused, and the meeting was adjourned so that Mr. Finkelberg could discuss the situation with Pfizer management.

The adjournment lasted for over an hour, during which time Mr. Finkelberg appeared to be talking intensely on his cell phone. It is worth noting that an employee has very few rights in an internal investigation, and employees at other companies have been fired simply for refusing to participate without a lawyer. Pfizer could very well have refused a tape recording. But now, when I had the interest of the press, Pfizer had to consider the public's reception of their actions. They wouldn't benefit from making a martyr out of me—just yet.

The interrogation resumed after Pfizer management finally relented and approved our tape recording of the meeting. I don't know what the questioning would have been like without that tape recorder, but it was contentious enough as it was. Mr. Finkelberg asked about almost every minute of my life from the time we had met last week. He even wanted to know where I had slept in Washington.

He also pressed me about my conversations with the senators and congressmen I met, and what they had said. The whole thing lasted a full day, and it felt pretty confrontational. At one point, his harrying questions made me so upset that I couldn't control myself and started shouting back at him. Mr. Finkelberg shook his head and shrunk in his seat—it was clear that my reaction made him feel very uncomfortable. My attorney asked for a break, which was immediately granted.

A few days later, Mr. Finkelberg sent his third letter, emphasizing that I *must* notify Pfizer before meeting with public officials. That was the same day that several congressmen sent an open letter to Pfizer's CEO and board of directors expressing their serious concern about Pfizer's intimidation of me as a direct result of my attendance at a proceeding before Congress.[1]

In their letter to Pfizer they condemned the legal inquiry, "If this is true, yesterday's interrogation, during which attorneys demanded details of private conversations with Members of Congress and their staffs, was clearly intended to intimidate Dr. Rost." It also stated, "It is the height of hypocrisy for a company that encourages its employees to engage in political matters to retaliate against an employee who is expressing his own policy views on his own time. Rost has been repeatedly encouraged, as an employee, to support political positions and to make specific political financial contributions."

A spokesman for Pfizer confirmed to the press that a meeting took place between an attorney for Pfizer and me and my legal counsel, "The meeting was professional and entirely consistent with Pfizer's policy regarding respect for employees,"[2] he said.

Blocking Pfizer

I was still trying to fulfill my duties as a Pfizer employee, so I replied to Mr. Finkelberg and told him, "I will make every effort to comply with your requests. I am concerned, however, that some of your demands are unreasonable and physically impossible to abide by."[3] I also wrote, "I get phone calls from journalists all the time, and I can't call Pfizer and notify them before picking up the phone, I don't even know if the journalist will ask me for any statements about reimportation."

I wanted to block him from continuing to interrogate me. My instinct told me that, since he absolutely didn't want to know about any other legal matters with Pfizer, it might be good for me if I *did* tell him about those matters. So I informed him that I was a witness in an ongoing criminal investigation and listed the statutes that stipulated that whoever retaliates against a witness shall be fined or imprisoned not more than 10 years.

I emphasized that "it is chilling for me to note that after senior management at Pfizer finds out that I am a witness in a criminal investigation, they hire you to ask me to start reporting on all my personal political activities and contacts with the press." I concluded by asking him respectfully to reformulate his request more narrowly so that I might be able to expediently comply with all of Pfizer's wishes.

I also decided that I should pull my invisible bosses into the situation. They had been hiding from sight for too long—people who were responsible for me and had isolated me, who would have to be more careful how they behaved if they knew about my contacts with law enforcement. So I informed them too, in a separate letter, that I was a witness in a criminal investigation.[4]

On October 4, I sent an e-mail to Ronald Chapman, Hank McKinnell, and Clark Finkelberg, in which I said, "It is your obligation to immediately terminate your ongoing investigation of my political opinions, the foundation for those opinions, and my past and future contacts with senators and members of Congress."[5]

I referred to one of Hank's e-mails and said, "Dr. McKinnell clearly encourages employees to vote and seek out their elected representatives, saying that 'Another way to participate in the political process is to help communicate about the work we do at Pfizer to federal, state and local candidates and public officials.' Your investigation of my political activity, in combination with this statement, indicates that Pfizer intimidates employees for the purpose of interfering with the right of employees to vote or to vote as they may choose." I ended the letter with, "Unless I hear otherwise I shall assume that your illegal investigation has been terminated."

How I Lost My Supervisors

The result of this was that I never heard from Mr. Finkelberg again, which was exactly what I had been hoping for. I am sure he is a nice guy with a family who loves him, but I didn't share that love. A week later, I got two surprising e-mails from my supervisors, Harry Otter and Ivana Fokker. They both wrote virtually identical messages, and said they understood that Mr. Finkelberg would be responding to me directly on behalf of the company—and then followed the interesting part.

Harry stated, "As I'm sure you are aware based on our absence of inter-action, I am not your supervisor. In fact, to the best of my recollection, I don't believe we have ever met."[6] And Ivana said, "As you know, I am not your supervisor. In fact, I'm not sure we've communicated since last year."[7]

I just loved it. Pfizer's people were so eager to distance themselves from me that they fell over each other running in the opposite direction. My response didn't take long to write.[8] I pointed out that they had both just gone on record and informed me that they were not my supervisors. Then I referred back to the e-mail sent by Wyler Jennings on April 17, 2003, which they had been copied on. Wyler had specifically instructed all of us that I would report to Harry and Ivana. I pointed out to the two of them that until now they had not sent me any communication that changed this relationship. I reminded Harry that since I had not met him, I had attempted to set up a meeting, but he never responded. Finally, I attached all my expense reports, which Harry had approved, and reminded him that his electronic signatures were on them. It was ridiculous for him to pretend that I had never reported to him.

I ended my letter advising them that if Pfizer had instructed them to write their misleading e-mails, they might want to consider hiring their own legal counsel. I tried to be helpful and informed them that, according to company by-laws, they would be reimbursed by Pfizer for this expense. Of course I didn't hear a word back. Later I wrote to them again to find out who my new supervisor was, but they didn't respond. I never heard from either one of them again. To the best of my knowledge, I became the only Pfizer employee without a boss.

NINETEEN

How Corrupt Is the Drug Industry?

SENATOR CHUCK GRASSLEY (R-IA), said in March of 2005, that "According to the Department of Justice, there are currently under seal in the neighborhood of 100 whistleblower cases involving allegations against over 200 drug companies. During the past four years, the [justice] department recovered nearly two and a half billion dollars from whistleblower cases against drug companies. Unfortunately, it appears that some drug companies are placing greed ahead of drug safety."[1] Senator Grassley also stated, "We've learned some fundamental points from these experiences. First, we're reminded again that whistleblowers are patriots. Think about the guts it takes to undermine your career, and to go against your supervisors at a huge federal agency, and in this case, the multi-billion-dollar drug companies. Whistleblowers are the rare birds who refuse to go along to get along. Their courage leads to the protection of public safety."

For obvious reasons, companies that have to pay hundreds of millions of dollars in fines and penalties may not be as enamored of whistleblowers as Senator Grassley. Lobbyists are actively working on weakening the laws that keep corporate crooks at bay.

So let's look at the facts. Let's find out how corrupt the drug industry really is. There is only one way to measure this and that is to review their public record: During the last five years more than half of the large drug companies have paid criminal and civil fines, amounting to billions of dollars. If an individual is convicted of a crime, we call him a criminal; however, if a company is convicted of a crime, what do we call it? We don't call it a criminal corporation, but perhaps we should.

I have to admit I felt great sadness writing this particular chapter. I have been proud of the drug industry's accomplishments, and most colleagues I have worked with have been honest, hard-working regular people. But when you look at the public record, these companies appear more like mob enterprises than law-abiding organizations. The only explanation I have is that money corrupts—again and again.

What I am about to demonstrate is not how bad things are. It is, likely, just the tip of the iceberg: The following are simply examples of those who got caught and convicted in spite of their law firms and political connections. So many companies wouldn't have paid such huge fines if something wasn't truly amiss. These cases also make me question my choice to spend all those years in the drug industry. Of course, if all the executives who do business the old-fashioned, honest way quit, there would be nothing left but underperforming crooks, trying to cheat their way to success.

TAP and AstraZeneca Pay Over a Billion Dollar in Fines

The biggest drug company fine ever paid was coughed up by TAP Pharmaceutical Products. In 2001, after a former TAP vice president of sales filed a False Claims Act complaint against the company, they agreed to pay $875 million to resolve criminal charges and civil liabilities in connection with their fraudulent drug pricing and marketing conduct of Lupron. This is a drug sold primarily for treatment of advanced prostate cancer. TAP agreed to plead guilty to a conspiracy to violate the Prescription Drug Marketing Act which included a $290-million criminal fine, the largest criminal fine ever in a health-care fraud prosecution. TAP also agreed to settle its False Claims Act liabilities and to pay $559.5 million to the U.S government for filing false and fraudulent claims with the Medicare and Medicaid programs and to settle its civil liabilities to the fifty states and the District of Columbia and to pay them $25.5 million for filing false and fraudulent claims.[2]

The False Claims Act is one of the government's strongest weapons against cheating corporations. If a corporation cheats the government out of money, then it has to pay up to triple damages. And there is a twist: The whistleblower may receive between 15 and 30 percent of the recovery. TAP also had to sign a "corporate integrity agreement" and comply with the terms of this sweeping document, which significantly changed the manner in which TAP supervised its marketing and sales staff. TAP is a joint venture, owned 50 percent by the U.S. drug company Abbot and 50 percent by the Japanese company Takeda.

This was not the first time Abbot was connected to corporate misbehavior. Back in 1999, they signed an FDA consent decree, paid a $100-million fine, and were forced to stop manufacturing and distributing many in-vitro diagnostic tests until manufacturing problems were corrected.[3] Then again in 2003 Abbott had to pay $382 million in the first combined civil settlement and criminal conviction arising from "Operation Headwaters," an undercover investigation by the FBI, the U.S. Postal Inspection Service, and the Office of the Inspector General for HHS. During this operation, various manufacturers offered kickbacks to undercover agents to purchase their products and then advised them how to fraudulently bill the government for those items. Out of the $382 million, $200 million were criminal fines.[4]

The same whistleblower who pointed his finger at TAP also accused AstraZeneca of similar misdeeds and filed a complaint against them. Based on that complaint, in 2003 AstraZeneca pleaded guilty to healthcare crimes and agreed to pay $355 million to resolve criminal charges and civil liabilities in connection with its drug pricing and marketing practices with regard to Zoladex, a drug sold for the treatment of prostate cancer. Of this amount, $266 million was recovered under the False Claims Act, and the remainder was levied as criminal fines.[5]

Douglas Durand, the former sales vice president at TAP who blew the whistle both at TAP and AstraZeneca, walked away with a cool $77 million for his role in the TAP settlement and another $47.5 million for the AstraZeneca settlement. He probably paid about 40 percent of these amounts to his law firm and perhaps another 30 percent in tax, but the net amount should sustain a comfortable lifestyle. It is worth noting, however, that these large amounts are the exception rather than the rule. Most whistleblowers walk away with nothing and often lose their jobs.

Pfizer Fined Hundreds of Millions

There were many more companies paying fines and signing corporate integrity agreements. In 2002 Pfizer agreed to pay $49 million and sign a corporate integrity agreement to settle allegations that Warner-Lambert, bought by Pfizer, had violated the False Claims Act.[6] The government alleged that Warner-Lambert fraudulently avoided paying a portion of the rebates owed to state and federal governments under the national drug Medicaid rebate program for the cholesterol-lowering drug Lipitor.

Pfizer was again forced to sign a corporate integrity agreement in 2004, while agreeing to pay $430 million to resolve civil and criminal charges that Warner-Lambert had defrauded Medicaid by engaging in an aggressive and complex scheme to illegally promote Neurontin, a drug indicated for epilepsy, for at least eleven off-label uses.[7] Among those uses were ADHD, mental illnesses, and a variety of pain conditions, including migraine headaches. The company was also alleged to have made kickbacks and payments to doctors in the form of trips to Puerto Rico, Florida, Hawaii, and elsewhere as an inducement for them to give speeches promoting the off-label use of the drugs, as well as paying doctors to "author" medical journal articles that were actually written by a medical-marketing firm.[8]

Of the total $430 million payout, $152 million settled the False Claims Act aspects of the case, and an additional $240 million represented criminal penalties. Another $38 million went to state consumer-protection agencies.

Bayer Pleads Guilty

In 2003 Bayer, a German company, pled guilty to violating the federal Prescription Drug Marketing Act, signed a corporate integrity agreement, and paid $257 million. This included a criminal fine of $5.6 million for overcharges involving its antibiotic Cipro and its high blood-pressure drug Adalat, and nearly $252 million in civil penalties under the False Claims Act.[9] Bayer's conduct was billed as "the largest Medicaid fraud in history."[10] The whistleblower in this case, Mr. Couto, died of pancreatic cancer before Bayer pled guilty. But this wasn't the first time Bayer had made fraudulent claims to the Medicaid program. Back in 2001, Bayer agreed to such a corporate integrity agreement, and agreed to pay $14 million for underpaying the Medicaid program.[11]

I've become pretty cynical due to my own experiences, but even I was shocked by what happened at Merck. In 2004, Merck's withdrawal of Vioxx resulted in a 27 percent drop in stock value and exposed the company to billions of dollars in liabilities. Some analysts estimated that this could eventually cost the company up to $50 billion.[12] And the Vioxx trials are not going the way Merck had hoped. Merck's legal problems in the spring of 2006 got a whole lot worse. A jury in New Jersey found that Merck had misled the Food and Drug Administration about the dangers of its painkiller Vioxx and acted "with wanton disregard for patients taking the drug." The jury awarded $9 million in punitive damages in addition to $4.5 million in compensatory damages to one plaintiff who had a heart attack in 2004 after taking Vioxx for four years. This means that Merck has lost two out of the four Vioxx cases that have gone to trial.[13]

Merck also faced other potential problems outside the personal-injury area. Many lawyers have said that it is likely that the company could also be sued by shareholders hurt financially by Merck's dropping stock price. There is already a securities case pending against Merck in federal court in New Orleans, alleging the company's stock price has been artificially inflated. Merck surely is in a world of hurt.[14]

But Vioxx wasn't the first time Merck had gotten into trouble. In a filing in its first quarter financial report in 2004 with the Securities and Exchange Commission, Merck revealed that the IRS had served the company with a "preliminary notice of deficiency."[15] The IRS asserted that the partnership Merck created, in 1993, to finance its acquisition of Medco was created to be a tax shelter. Merck claimed that the partnership was necessary to finance the acquisition and was not created solely to avoid taxes. If the IRS prevails, Merck could owe $2.04 billion, excluding any penalties the IRS might impose.

Glaxo CEO: "I'm No Mother Theresa"

Another company with major tax problems is GlaxoSmithKline. The company is facing a demand for a whopping $7.8 billion from the IRS in backdated taxes and interest—enough to almost wipe out a year's profits at this big drug manufacturer from the United Kingdom. The IRS claims that more of the firm's profits made on sales in the U.S. should be taxed here in the U.S. [16] GlaxoSmithKline—not surprisingly—is contesting the claim. But the company doesn't have problems just with the IRS; it has put aside over a billion dollars to cover potential payments for its disputes with tax authorities around the world. The firm's last annual report states that it has "issues" with tax authorities in the U.S., the U.K., Japan, and Canada.[17]

Perhaps it shouldn't be surprising to know that when shareholders questioned GlaxoSmithKline's CEO about his pay package in 2003, Jean-Pierre Garnier proudly declared to the press, "I am not Mother Teresa." [18] In fact, this company has a long history of getting in trouble with the law. Back in 1997, one of the companies that later formed GlaxoSmithKline paid $325 million to resolve federal and state fraud claims alleging overcharges to the Medicare, Medicaid, and other health care programs, one of the two largest False Claims Act settlements of that time.[19] In 2003, the company had to sign a corporate integrity agreement and pay a civil fine of $88 million for overcharging Medicaid in a False Claims Act case involving its anti-depressant Paxil and the nasal-allergy spray Flonase.[20]

The following year, the New York State Attorney General, Eliot Spitzer, sued GlaxoSmithKline over unpublished studies showing lack of efficacy of Paxil in children; Spitzer claimed that the company withheld information from doctors about the negative results of clinical trials it conducted on the use of Paxil in children.[21] Spitzer's lawsuit alleged that GlaxoSmithKline published only one of five studies it conducted on the impact of Paxil on children and suppressed the negative results of the other studies. An internal memo said that the company intended to manage "the dissemination of data in order to minimize any potential negative commercial impact."[22] Garnier fought back in the press. "Can a company control the millions, and I mean millions, of memoranda written by, in our case, 110,000 people? What are the odds that stupid memos were written? What are the odds that memos asking the company to do things against company policy will be written? The odds are 100 percent! Of course we didn't follow this advice. Of course we didn't selectively publicize the data. This is not a smoking gun. It's a stupid memo and there are lots of stupid memos in every company's file and it is really unfair to look at the company's action through the small hole of one memo written among thousands and thousands in 1998. I do regret that those memos exist, but I'm not going to lose sleep over the fact."[23]

Garnier *didn't* mention the billions of dollars owed to tax authorities around the globe, nor the hundreds of millions GlaxoSmithKline and its heritage companies had already been forced to pay in fines and settlements. Nor were "stupid memos" the reason U.S. Marshals seized millions of Paxil tablets in 2005. The FDA took this rare move because GlaxoSmithKline repeatedly failed to correct problems cited during 2003 and 2004 inspections of their manufacturing plant in Puerto Rico. The company subsequently signed a FDA consent decree promising to rectify their substandard manufacturing practices.[24]

Later in 2005 the Justice Department announced that Glaxo had paid "over $150 million to resolve allegations that the company violated the False Claims Act through fraudulent drug pricing and marketing."[25]

Let's stop for a second and imagine that GlaxoSmithKline was a private individual—and that Mr. Glaxo was accused of owing huge taxes around the world, had paid many large fines and even had to sign an integrity agreement *and* a consent decree, and responded by saying "I'm no mother Teresa"; how would we view such a person, in light of all this information? No one would want to have anything to do with him. HE would be regarded as a mobster, an outcast. But those rules don't apply to rich corporations.

Bristol-Myers Squibb Invents $1.5 Billion Sales

Pharmaceutical companies don't just run afoul of the False Claims Act and the tax man. In 2004 the Securities and Exchange Commission (SEC) ordered Bristol-Myers Squibb to pay $150 million to settle charges that it inflated its revenue by $1.5 billion in 2000 and 2001. The penalty was one of the largest levied against a company accused of accounting fraud.[26] The settlement concluded a two-year SEC investigation of the company, but the bad news for Bristol-Myers Squibb didn't stop there.

A separate criminal investigation by the U.S. Attorney General's office in New Jersey resulted in the indictment of two executives: The former senior vice president and chief financial officer, and the former executive vice president and president of the Bristol-Myers Squibb's world-wide medicines group. Both were charged with securities fraud and conspiracy to commit securities fraud, for planning and executing channel stuffing at the company.[27]

The company also agreed to pay $300 million to shareholders and to enter a deferred-prosecution agreement. This allowed Christopher Christie, the U.S. Attorney for the District of New Jersey, to reach an agreement that he personally would oversee the company and keep the business viable and clean. Interesting to note is that the Mr. Christie, according to the *Wall Street Journal*, said he "didn't impose fines on the company because he didn't want to hurt the company or its shareholders and employees."[28] It's great to be a corporation, isn't it? Imagine a judge telling a criminal that he doesn't want to impose any fines, because he doesn't want to hurt the crook . . .

Wyeth Signs FDA Consent Agreement

GlaxoSmithKline wasn't the only company that couldn't manufacture its own drugs according to good manufacturing standards. In 2000, Wyeth signed an FDA Consent Decree, paid $30 million, and agreed to a series of measures aimed at ensuring that their Marietta, Pennsylvania, and Pearl River, New York, facilities were manufacturing in compliance with FDA's good manufacturing practice regulations.[29]

Wyeth's biggest problem, however, was that they had been forced to set aside $21.1 billion to settle "fen-phen" cases after pulling the diet drugs Pondimin and Redux off the market in 1997. These drugs contained the same active substance, which had caused heart-valve and lung damage in some of the approximately 5.8 million Americans who took them.[30]

Schering-Plough Pays Record Fine

In 2002, Schering-Plough, another major pharmaceutical manufacturer, also signed a FDA consent decree and paid a $500-million fine, the highest monetary settlement in FDA history.[31] They had violated manufacturing regulations at the firm's New Jersey and Puerto Rico plants. The decree affected how the company manufactured about 125 different prescription and over-the-counter drugs at their Puerto Rico and New Jersey facilities. As part of the decree, the company also agreed to suspend manufacturing seventy-three other products.

There was more to come for Schering-Plough. In 2004, the company paid $345 million to resolve criminal and civil liabilities for illegal marketing of Claritin. The settlement agreement included a criminal fine of $52.5 million for violating the Anti-Kickback Statute. They were also forced to sign a corporate integrity agreement.[32]

This is a company that has fought against reimportation of drugs, claiming it could jeopardize patient safety, and it can't even manufacture its own drugs safely.

Serono Executives Charged with Conspiracy

In October 2005, Serono Laboratories of Switzerland agreed to pay a total of $704 million to resolve criminal charges and civil liabilities in connection with their marketing of Serostim, an AIDS drug. They also agree to plead guilty to two counts of criminal conspiracy. Not long before, in December 2004, the Regional Director for Sales in New York pled guilty to a marketing conspiracy. In April 2005, four other Serono sales and marketing executives were indicted on charges of conspiracy and offering to pay illegal remunerations. These charges are still pending.[33]

Eli Lilly Latest Company to Bite the Dust

In December 2005, Indianapolis based company Eli Lilly agreed to plead guilty and to pay $36 million in connection with its illegal promotion of its pharmaceutical drug Evista. This drug is approved by the FDA for the prevention and treatment of osteoporosis in post-menopausal women; however, since sales didn't go very well, the company decided to embark on off-label promotion. The Justice Department claims that sales representatives were trained to prompt or bait questions by doctors in order to promote Evista for unapproved uses and that Eli Lilly encouraged sales representatives to promote Evista by sending unsolicited medical letters to promote the drug for unapproved uses to doctors on their sales routes. The company also organized a "market research summit" during which Evista was discussed with physicians for unapproved uses. In short, Eli Lilly bit the dust and proved themselves to be nothing but bad marketers trying to compensate by cheating.[34]

Crime Pays for Big Pharma

Although our drug companies have paid billions in damages for their violations, many violations may never be discovered. Each one of these pharmaceutical companies creates many billions in profits every year—and from a strict profit-and-loss perspective, crime often pays for corporations. Neurontin, for instance, had sales of over $2 billion per year and Pfizer only paid a $430 million fine. The government estimates that 94 percent of those sales revenues were for off-label purposes. [35]

Surprisingly, in spite of their admitted criminal and fraudulent conduct, not everyone agrees that drug companies should have to pay these penalties, *or* that they are guilty as charged.

Forbes Comes to the Rescue

An example of this opposing view is a 2005 cover story in *Forbes*, with the headline "The Dark Side of Whistleblowing."[36] *Forbes* not only tried to make a villain of the whistleblower who caused TAP and AstraZeneca to pay over a billion dollars—"Instead of trying to fix the problem, he spent seven months gathering evidence of supposed fraud"—but also called into question the False Claims Act:

> In the post-Enron era, these self-appointed do-gooders are granted breathless audiences by Congress, extolled on national television and lauded by *Time* magazine as Persons of the Year. But some whistleblowers are motivated by greed, willing to stretch the truth for profit...The government is often a willing accomplice, keen to look tough and cash in. It tars targets with bad press and threatens to levy fines many times the size of its own purported losses. If a company refuses to settle, the feds can move to ban it from federal business even before getting so much as an indictment. Most times companies settle, whether they are guilty or not."

The executives at TAP, who had paid one of the biggest fines in corporate history, close to a billion dollars, pled guilty to crimes, and signed a corporate integrity agreement, had perhaps been *blackmailed* by our government. So, perhaps they were actually the *good guys* and the nasty prosecutors were the *bad guys*.

In fairness to *Forbes*, it should be noted that they weren't the first ones to put forward the theory that many corporations have simply been taken advantage of. Thomas Watkins, TAP's president at the time, claimed that TAP had agreed to pay the big fine only because the government had threatened to end federal reimbursements for Lupron, worth half a billion dollars a year. This comment enraged William Young, the chief U.S. District Court judge in Boston, who forbade TAP from making further claims of innocence. "I don't want some P.R. flack saying this is all just a big misunderstanding."

But that is exactly what the *Forbes* article suggested. And just in case the reader of *Forbes* would have any problem sympathizing with the convicted company, the editorial bent only got stronger and the article ended, "By the time the legal holes, logical leaps and inaccuracies in the case were revealed in the criminal trial last year, TAP had been shaken down."

And in this systematic "shakedown" the government has recouped over $17 billion from convicted corporations due to the False Claims Act. As taxpayers and employees, we should be pleased. The fact that some embarrassed executives, together with the well-respected business magazine *Forbes,* disagree may not be surprising.

TWENTY

FDA Secrets

IT IS SAD TO OBSERVE CORRUPT CORPORATIONS, but even worse to note a breakdown in the oversight of these companies. When the FDA convened an advisory board in 2005 to determine if the drugs in the Vioxx-class—Celebrex, Bextra, and Vioxx—were safe and should stay on the market, it was discovered that ten of the thirty-two government drug advisers who endorsed continued marketing of these blockbuster pain-control pills had previously consulted for the pharmaceutical companies.[1]

In fact, of the thirty votes cast by these ten "tainted" panel members, they voted twenty-eight times in favor of keeping the drugs on the market. Among the sixty-six votes cast by the remaining twenty-two members of the panel, only about half of those votes favored keeping the drugs on the market.[2] Because the panel included these scientists who had taken drug-industry money, the panel voted to keep *all* three drugs on the market—even Vioxx, which had already been taken off the market by Merck.[3] If the ten drug company advisers had *not* cast their votes, the panel would have voted fourteen to eight that Vioxx should not return to the market and twelve to eight that Bextra should be withdrawn.[4] The ten advisers with company ties voted nine to one to keep Bextra on the market and nine to one for Vioxx's return.

Eight of the ten panel members said in later interviews that their past relationships with the drug companies had "not influenced their votes."[5] Nevertheless, says Dr. Sheldon Krimsky, a science policy expert at Tufts University, "such conflicts are common on F.D.A. advisory panels. The agency often conceals these conflicts, and studies have shown that, taken as a whole, money does influence scientific judgments."[6] In the end, the FDA made the unusual decision not to follow the panel's recommendation, and decided to remove Bextra from the market.

And while the FDA enjoys a fine reputation with the public—77 percent claim they are somewhat confident or confident in the FDA's ability to ensure the safety of prescription drugs in the U.S.—the same confidence doesn't exist within the FDA, among the people who should really know.[7]

FDA Staffers Don't Trust the FDA

An internal FDA survey demonstrated that a majority of the scientists surveyed—66 percent—lacked confidence in the "ability of the agency to adequately monitor the safety of prescription drugs on the market."[8] This unpublished internal survey was conducted in 2002 by the Health and Human Services Office of Inspector General. The survey also revealed that 18 percent of FDA scientists had been "pressured to approve or recommend approval for a [new drug application] despite reservations about the safety, efficacy, or quality of the drug."

36 percent of the scientists in the survey said they were only somewhat confident or not confident at all in the FDA's decisions regarding drug safety. Finally, when it came to drug effectiveness, 22 percent of scientists said they were only somewhat confident or not confident at all in the agency's decisions.[9] The results are even more remarkable considering that almost 400 scientists participated in the survey and knew they could be traced by their management, since the survey wasn't anonymous.

The survey supported the allegations made by the FDA's own

whistleblower, Dr. David Graham, who testified before the U.S. Senate at the end of 2004 about how the FDA treated Merck with kid gloves and was reluctant to remove Vioxx from the market. Graham told the committee he was intimidated by FDA officials after a study he conducted showed Vioxx increased the risk of heart attack. Twenty-two members of Congress signed a letter to acting FDA commissioner Lester Crawford. The letter said the members wanted "to express our strong dismay at recent reports about efforts taken by some at FDA to discredit and smear Dr. Graham."[10] They added, "This shameful behavior by management cannot continue and we demand you put a stop to it." Dr. Crawford was confirmed as the new FDA commissioner; however, he resigned under mysterious circumstances after two months, in September 2005. In April it was reported that a grand jury had begun a critical investigation of Dr. Crawford amid accusations of financial improprieties and making false statements to Congress.

Electronic Surveillance?

Dr. Graham's story had several similarities to my own, and I know that encouragement is important when someone is standing up against his superiors, so I wrote a brief e-mail congratulating him on his senate testimony about Vioxx. Later I also sent another e-mail explaining some of the legalities that could help Graham defend himself against the FDA. As I sometimes do with important e-mails, I used a service which tracks when my mail is opened, for how long, and on which computer. The mail wasn't just opened on one computer, labeled "wallsand-pub.fda.gov (150.148.0.31)," but also on two additional FDA computers, named "wallwhale-pub.fda.gov (150.148.0.27)" and walltiger-pub.fda.gov (150.148.0.28)." I suspected that someone else was looking at Dr. Graham's mail, so I sent a warning to him and told him what I had discovered.

I also put a tracer on my second e-mail. Less than an hour after

Dr. Graham had opened this mail, my message was opened on yet another computer within the FDA, called "wall3-pub.fda.gov (150.148.0.65)"

I figured that Dr. Graham had sent my message with his own comments straight to the acting FDA commissioner, Dr. Lester Crawford. But I didn't know what his computer was named, so I sent my own e-mail to Dr. Crawford, with no message, but with a tracer attached. And lo and behold, the computer which opened that message was "wall3-pub.fda.gov (150.148.0.65)," the same computer my message to Dr. Graham had also been opened on. Then I also noted that Dr. Graham forwarded one of my messages to someone in the U.S. Senate. I presumed that was to Senator Grassley, who had helped him speak out against his employer.

None of this is conclusive proof that the FDA monitored Dr. Graham, but it sure made me wonder if Pfizer was not the only organization keeping close tabs on its employees.

TWENTY-ONE

Going on the Offense

I DIDN'T KNOW WHEN OR HOW MY FIGHT with Pfizer would end. Looking ahead, I knew I could never compete against Pfizer and its resources; however, if I mobilized other powerful entities, such as the government, then perhaps I stood a chance. To do that, I needed to prove that this wasn't about me, that it truly was about illegal business practices.

As I thought about the situation, I realized that the best way to maintain my credibility would be to have other people corroborate my story. However, all the employees who could have done that had signed release agreements saying they would never sue Pfizer; in fact, they would have to cooperate with Pfizer if Pfizer ever got into legal trouble. It positioned my friends as potential adversaries, a devilish set-up. But not everyone had been fired; some others were also in limbo. It appeared as if Antonio Berzeli, who headed my former U.S. research group, was in a situation similar to mine. He hadn't been fired; he didn't do much work; and he surely wasn't spending much time in his office. But he was still a Pfizer employee.

Another Outcast within Pfizer

I decided to contact him and soon found out that, like me, he had been deliberately marginalized and put into employment "purgatory." His only job remained firing people in his rapidly-diminishing department. While Pfizer had given him a nine-month retention agreement, it appeared as if Antonio would be fired when that agreement was over. Was it any coincidence that Antonio, like me, had been presenting our concerns about illegal marketing at that October 2002 meeting at Pfizer headquarters? Or that virtually everyone from that meeting was gone? Like me, Antonio had raised serious legal and ethical issues concerning the marketing of Genotropin, particularly how Pharmacia treated doctors lavishly in order to generate sales.

A few phone calls later, I had convinced Antonio that he should retain my lawyer. And it didn't take Jon long until he had determined that Antonio's situation was a mirror of mine, and just as potentially damaging for Pfizer. With Antonio on board, I would have Pfizer on a tight leash, at least for the time being. Shortly thereafter Pfizer agreed to extend my tolling agreement and signed a tolling agreement with Antonio. With two people from the same department being treated the same way now sharing the same lawyer, the pressure on Pfizer was increasing.

Eliot Spitzer Gets Involved

But I knew better than to sit back and enjoy my most recent victory. I preferred to be in control of my own destiny rather than sit in the wings and wait. Why should I put my life on hold because Pfizer refused to give me anything reasonable to do and declined to have any discussions with my attorney? My forced idleness was making me anxious, so I decided to continue my search for additional government support. There is always something more that can be done, and I certainly had the time to consider my options.

Then it hit me—there was no one so feared in the industry as Eliot Spitzer, New York's Attorney General. He had taken on industry after industry and usually wrangled settlements out of the most hardcore executives. He had recently challenged GlaxoSmithKline using an obscure consumer-protection law, and made them post all their clinical trials for the public to see. If I could get Spitzer interested, I would have Pfizer tied in knots.

I began e-mailing Spitzer information on the Genotropin situation. Though I didn't hear back, by using my e-mail tracking service, I could see that the messages were opened. Then one day in August, Jon Green forwarded a message to me, which he had received from Antonio. Pfizer had received a letter from Spitzer's office wanting specific documents regarding the promotion of a number of products, among them Genotropin, and we were requested by Pfizer "not destroy any documents concerning research on or marketing or sales" of those products. The memo from Pfizer was signed by my old correspondent, legal compliance officer Arthur Richardson.[1]

Shortly after learning about Spitzer's request, I wrote him a letter in which I revealed the internal allegations of misconduct within Pfizer's senior management, as well as the damning results from Pfizer's own employee survey, in which 30 percent of the employees didn't agree with the statement "Pfizer management demonstrates honest, ethical behavior."[2]

This time I got a rapid reaction from Spitzer's office. Peter Drago, Spitzer's director of public information as well as Joe Baker, Bureau Chief of Spitzer's Health Care Bureau contacted me[3] and it didn't take long until I was asked to meet with Rose Firestein, Assistant Attorney General, Bureau of Consumer Frauds & Protection.[4] She had been the one responsible for filing Spitzer's consumer-fraud lawsuit against Glaxo for allegedly engaging in "repeated and persistent fraud by concealing and failing to disclose to physicians certain information about Paxil."

Rose seated me in a cramped conference room, located in a building next to the New York stock exchange. I sensed immediately that she was sharp—I wouldn't ever want to be an executive standing in her way. New York consumer-fraud law scared corporations, she told me, because the prosecutor didn't have to prove intent to commit fraud—just that New York's residents had been defrauded. That made her job all the more interesting. I am not someone who generally adores persons in power, but Eliot Spitzer and his department had impressed me—where other regulators and law enforcement agents have sat on their hands, he had stepped in and gotten results. Having his department looking into Pfizer's issues felt very reassuring.

The New Jersey Justice Department Calls a Meeting

I knew I had to keep as many fronts open as I could. Spitzer was responsible for New York state law, not federal law, so I also wrote an e-mail to Mr. Christopher Christie, nominated by President George Bush to be the United States Attorney for the Justice Department in New Jersey. I told him that I believed that I had been subject to intimidation and illegal political pressure by my employer Pfizer, aimed at stopping my lawful political activity conducted in my private time. I also informed him that this included a written request to inform Pfizer of all my future contacts with Senators and Members of Congress in advance of such meetings.[5]

I sent a couple of additional e-mails right after this one, showing the pressure Pfizer's CEO exerted upon Pfizer employees through e-mails and phone calls, including requests to vote for certain issues, contact congressmen, and donate money to Pfizer's political action committee, as well as directly to political campaigns. My point was that Hank couldn't ask his employees to become politically active and then turn around and retaliate when they did.

The following day I got a phone call from Christie's right-hand man, James Nobile, chief of the special prosecutions division at the New Jersey Justice Department. He asked me to come in right away, and the next day I drove to Newark, where the Justice Department was located.

I remembered this federal building well; it was the place where I had received my American citizenship ten years earlier...an eternity ago. Now, although I had accomplished much of what I had dreamt of that day, I lived in this strange, surreal world of lawyers, litigation, criminal investigations, and other unpleasant matters. It was weird to think back on those early days; one supervisor in my first pharmaceutical job had actually told me that I needed to be more assertive—if only he could see me now. I was ready to give Mr. Nobile all I had.

James Nobile turned out to be a very polite man, with an exacting knowledge of federal laws and statutes. He brought with him Stanley Beet, a criminal investigator. Stan reminded me of the kind of dependable and reassuring police lieutenant made famous in so many movies. Jim asked for my entire story and went through the documents I brought with me. He focused on laws that made it illegal to dissuade anyone to appear before Congress and Pfizer's letter to a number of congressmen, as well as their investigation of me before going to Capitol Hill. He was also very interested in determining exactly where, physically, I had delivered my speech. He was satisfied when it turned out to be the Dirksen Senate Office building.

There was a question if my appearance would really qualify as "attending or testifying in an official proceeding before Congress." Additionally, I had not been scared enough by Pfizer to be kept away from my engagement, so he felt he did not have enough to proceed. But before I left, Jim asked me to notify him immediately if I encountered any more harassment from Pfizer. Little did I expect that I would be visiting him again only a few months later.

TWENTY-TWO

The Dirty Little Secret

A FLURRY OF INVITATIONS FOLLOWED MY SPEAKING engagement on Capitol Hill. I testified before the New York City Council, the Maryland Senate, the Maryland House of Delegates, and the Vermont Senate. I was also invited to several press conferences, among them, one with Governor Kernan in Indiana.

The experience in Indianapolis was unique. As soon as I arrived at the airport, Governor Kernan's aides informed me that the governor wanted to take a somewhat low-key approach to drug importation and call upon congress to act before he did anything locally. The biggest obstacle he faced in Indianapolis was the city's dominant company, pharmaceutical powerhouse Eli Lilly. This was a company town, with virtually everyone having a relative who worked at Eli Lilly or having shared in the company's largesse and charitable work. To make matters worse, Governor Kernan went into the election trailing his opponent, the likeable Mitch Daniels, a former Eli Lilly executive. I had expected an opportunity to pound not only on Mitch Daniels, but also Eli Lilly. Governor Kernan, however, would have none of that. He was very concerned about angering the mighty corporation that practically owned his constituents.

Eli Lilly's Surprise

I had a section in my speech that I had tailored specifically for this opportunity:

People have a hard time with honesty. Lilly's CEO Sidney Taurel already blames reimportation for his company's poor perform- ance, when he has no one to blame but himself. According to Reuters, last week Taurel said his company was 'cutting costs, partly in reaction to the looming threat of U.S. price controls and the import of cheaper medicines from abroad.'[1] Lilly's stock has dropped 30 percent in six months, not because of reimportation, but because of how Mr. Taurel runs his company. Some may ask why I have chosen to talk publicly about reimportation. Because contrary to what Mr. Taurel thinks, the free market works.

I was asked to delete that section from my speech, as well as tone down several other parts. But things didn't get any better from there. We left the imposing state house in the governor's dark blue car for a local senior center, where the press conference was going to take place. Everything looked calm and normal; the state's collective broadcast industry had gathered, along with many print journalists.

We started the press conference, and then something unexpected happened. A gentleman jumped up and declared that he was a retiree who just happened to have worked for Eli Lilly. He then proceeded to lash out *against* reimportation in front of the rolling television cameras.

Governor Kernan didn't move a finger, nor did he point out that the man was completely uninvited. Later, on the evening news, all channels covered the man's comments with restrained glee. I had become used to rave reviews from reporters, but the Indianapolis news anchors clearly were in the hands of Eli Lilly, and the company got extensive time for a rebuttal. Clearly, Governor Kernan had chal- lenges. Not surprisingly, he lost the election to Mitch Daniels.

Home Run in Montana

My experience at a press conference in Montana was quite different. Democrat Brian Schweitzer, who ran for governor with a Republican running mate, didn't apologize to anyone about drug importation. Already, back in 1999, he had shown courage and willingness to help Montana's citizens get lower-priced medicines. At that time, few talked about this issue, but Mr. Schweitzer had traveled with seniors across the border before everyone else started. He loved it when I said about his opponent, "Brown says the issue of importation is 'not relevant' to a governor's race. That is like saying people dying is not relevant to a governor's race."

In fact, I couldn't think of anything that was more relevant. And I wasn't alone. Eleven Republican and Democratic governors were moving forward with helping their citizens and pharmacists import safe lower-priced medicines. Governors were leading the way in this fight. You get a governor who is against reimportation, you get a state where people will die—people who could have stayed alive if they had the money for drugs. This is not a Republican or Democratic issue. I don't belong to either party. This is about life or death.

Schweitzer found that the public agreed, easily defeating his opponent to become the new governor of Montana.

Writing an Op-Ed for the *New York Times*

In the middle of all this, congressman Sander's office suggested that I write an op-ed for the *New York Times* on drug importation and, on the weekend before the presidential election, October 30, 2004, the *New York Times* published my piece, "Medicines without Borders."[2]

I have a confession to make. I am a drug company executive who believes we should legalize the reimportation of prescription drugs. I know that I have a different opinion from that of my employer on this matter, but to me, importation of drugs is about much more than money; it is about saving American lives.

I went through all the facts in favor of drug importation, and finally ended it, "I have another confession to make. Americans are dying without the appropriate drugs because my industry and Congress are more concerned about protecting astronomical profits for conglomerates than they are about protecting the health of Americans."

Of course I accept that business only has one purpose—to make money. But when you're in the business of saving lives, you also have to consider your bigger obligation to humanity. You can't maintain your profits if you don't care about the health of your patients.

It didn't take long until I got the reaction from Pfizer's employees. One lady wrote a very simple message. "I was very disappointed to see your ideas in the NY Times this weekend." I wrote her back and told her that she shouldn't be disappointed; my op-ed had been the newspaper's fourth most e-mailed story.[3]

Doctors Boycott Pfizer Sales Reps

Around this time, news also broke that a group of doctors in Santa Fe had banned Pfizer representatives from its offices because of the company's treatment of me. Dr. Paul Kovnat, one of the doctors in the group, was quoted in the *Albuquerque Journal*, "When you see this and you feel like you're a part of what they're doing and they're at the office, we wanted to speak out."[4] Dr. Kovnat also added that he had to order Pfizer sales reps out of the office several times since banning them. Additionally, the physician's group agreed that they wouldn't prescribe Pfizer drugs if suitable generic drugs were available.

Pfizer is a *very* sales oriented company and these events shook them up. Their worst nightmare would be a national boycott of their products. According to the *Albuquerque Journal*, Pfizer said the company had "several products of great value to patients" for problems such as high cholesterol, cancer, high blood pressure, and glaucoma. Attempting to minimize the significance of their actions, the spokesman claimed that the Santa Fe doctors were the first to take such an action. "We believe it would be unfortunate if patients were denied those therapies based on this current situation with Dr. Rost."

The paper also described when Dr. Kovnat ordered the Pfizer reps to leave the physician group's waiting room. "This is my house, and I get to control what's in my house, and I don't like what you're doing and I don't want you in my house."

This was a dangerous situation for me. I was speaking out in favor of drug importation, not against Pfizer. While I was thankful for anyone supporting me, I couldn't endorse a boycott of Pfizer products. Pfizer had attacked me personally, but I had no intention of doing the same to them.

The most precarious moment came when the journalist who wrote that article called and asked for my comments. To make sure that there were absolutely no misunderstandings I wrote a follow-up e-mail to her, saying, ". . . since I'm not allowed to speak of Pfizer or their business, we have to be careful how I'm quoted on this, i.e. to say that 'I'm humbled and gracious for people taking action and speaking out on my behalf' is OK, but to directly refer to the current action and say or intimate that, 'Dr. Rost approves boycotting Pfizer' would be incorrect.'" The journalist responded affirmatively, "Thanks for the follow-up note and I understand the subtlety of not being allowed to directly comment on this particular action. I'll make it clear in my story that you did not speak directly about the doctors and use your note as a guide."[5]

The next day the story was in the paper with the bold headline: "Pfizer Exec Thankful for Doctors' Boycott."[6] This was exactly what I had asked them not to write. No matter what precautions, it is impossible to guarantee what will show up in print.

Pfizer Lawyers Trailing Me

But let's go back to my favorite lawyer at Pfizer, Arthur Richardson, whom I really did like. I discovered that he was on my trail when I was preparing to hold a speech at a web conference with a group of drug company executives from across the world. On their screens they saw the face of Dr Eshetu Wondemagegnehu, the World Health Organization's leading expert on counterfeit medicines, as well as my picture. As the presentations continued they could also see our slides.

Before the meeting day, I asked the organizers to give me the names and titles of the audience. At first they balked, but when I reminded them that at any regular meeting you can see your audience, they relented and sent over an Excel sheet with the titles of everyone who had signed up. On line number forty-seven, I found "Assistant General Counsel, Pfizer, Inc."

There was no doubt in my mind that the lawyer was Arthur Richardson, and I imagined that he might be surrounded by people from Partland & Longhorn, perhaps a few private investigators and lots of machinery to record my speech. Interestingly, there was also someone with the title "director, investigations," from my prior employer, Wyeth, on the roster.

Perhaps I should have felt flattered, but in a way it was almost pathetic the way they hounded me and tried to catch me making a mistake. I decided to send all the snoops and investigators and lawyers a straightforward message at the end of my speech.

My Personal Message to Pfizer's Lawyers

When I had completed my main speech, I continued, "And now for a personal message to the lawyers and investigators, who are right now recording and writing down every word I say to try to find something that you can use against me—you know exactly who you are. You should be even more ashamed. I'd like you to ask yourself, do you want to simply continue to hunt someone trying to do the right thing, or do you want to make a difference. Do you think you're going to proudly tell your grandchildren that 'I stopped reimportation, and I made that guy Peter Rost really shut up.' Or do you think you'd be happier telling your children that you made a difference in the world, you made your company change its ways. That you saved people, that you brought drugs to everyone and not just the ones who could afford it. And don't give me the line about our industry's indigent programs. If they worked, one third of the uninsured wouldn't have gone without drugs they needed.

Many of you do know, deep down in your heart, that legalized reimportation is the right thing to do, for our business and our patients. Ever watched a hurricane? Some trees bend and survive, others are stiff and break. Our industry will break if we continue to fight this issue, if we're not part of the solution. I doubled sales by dropping prices. I saw the wave coming and I decided to surf and not fight it and drown. And it paid off for my business. I want to work with the industry, not against it. Our industry is on its way to disaster, and someone needs to speak up. Someone needs to tell it like it is. And that is what I'm trying to do."

The Dirty Little Secret

But I wasn't satisfied with just speaking at meetings, political rallies, and press conferences. The *New York Times* op-ed had made me realize that I could reach a lot of people through the written word rather than relying on others to repeat what I had said. And then, when I read an op-ed in the *Wall Street Journal* by Hank McKinnell, which started off saying, "The American health-care system is the best in the world," I just had to respond. So I wrote an op-ed in the *Los Angeles Times* under the headline, "Big Pharma's Dirty Little Secret."[7]

My point was that most people *think* the American healthcare system is the best in the world, but that this isn't really true. It is certainly the best system for drug companies, which can charge the highest prices in the world to some U.S. consumers. And it is a pretty good system for hospitals, insurance companies, and others that deliver healthcare services. Americans spend about twice as much per person for healthcare as do Canadians, Japanese, or Europeans, according to the World Health Organization. But it's not a good system for

American citizens. The U.S. has shorter life expectancies and higher infant and child mortality rates than Canada, Japan, and all of Western Europe except Portugal, according to the WHO.

Our dirty little secret is that the drug industry already sells its products, right here in the U.S., at the same low prices charged in Canada and Europe. It's done through rebates. These are given to those with enough power to negotiate drug prices, such as the Veterans Administration. A 2001 study by the consumer advocacy group Public Citizen found that drug companies' favorite customers paid just a little over half the retail price. This leaves the 67 million Americans without insurance to pay cash, with no rebates, at double the prices paid by the most-favored customers. The fight against reimportation of drugs is a fight to continue to charge our uninsureds full price while giving everyone else a rebate.

TWENTY-THREE

What the Government Tried to Hide

By THE END OF DECEMBER 2004, the Department of Health and Human Services came out with their report on drug importation. The report admitted that it would be possible to safely import drugs on a large scale, but claimed that establishing such a system wouldn't be cost effective.[1] The report also concluded that such a system would harm pharmaceutical companies' research and development efforts. The report was required by the new Medicare law, and had been developed by a thirteen-member panel led by U.S. Surgeon General Richard Carmona. Not surprisingly, the panel consisted of many representatives from several government agencies that oppose prescription drug reimportation.

The headlines in the major newspapers told the story:

"HHS Report: Drug Imports Likely Won't Save Money."[2]

"Importing Drugs Safely is Too Costly, Panel Says."[3]

"Legalizing Drug Imports Not Worth It."[4]

"Bush Panel Sees Scant Savings in Drug Imports."[5]

These comments were based on the fact that the report said that "total savings to drug buyers from legalized commercial importation would be 1 to 2 percent of total drug spending." But if this were true, reimportation of drugs would never take off. Why, then, I wondered, would the drug industry spend so much money fighting this plan? What was it that the drug companies knew, that the

Department of Health and Human Services didn't want the public to understand? The answer was that the data in the report didn't support the conclusions.

Numbers Hidden in the HHS Report

The HHS report actually indicated the possibility of saving much more money. And this also explained the drug industry's fear of importation. The department's conclusion was built upon the premise—as stated in the report—that "imported drugs may be around 12 percent of total use . . . because drug companies have incentives to impede exports." This assumption didn't take into account that reimportation bills would make it illegal for drug companies to artificially limit supply of drugs to other countries in an effort to reduce reimportation—something the drug companies were keenly aware of but the HHS completely ignored.

The second and more important faulty premise was that U.S. drug buyers would get discounts of only 20 percent or less, with the rest of the price difference going to commercial importers. This statement can be contrasted with a chart in the report showing that U.S. retail drug prices are often 100 percent higher than in Europe.[6]

So this premise assumed unprecedented price gouging by importers and a complete lack of competition among them. Of course, the drug industry knew that is not how the free market works, but the Department of Health and Human Services feigned ignorance.

Let's now do the analysis of savings possible in the United States based on the data in the report. We know that according to the HHS report drug prices in Europe are about 50 percent lower than in the United States. We also know that European drugs are traded profitably from one European country to the other when the price differential is just 10 percent, so let's assume that we get a 40 percent discount.

Then we take the report's premise that imported drugs may be around 12 percent of total use and compare that with what is going on in Europe. In the U.K. for instance, imported drugs account for

17.6 percent of pharmaceutical sales. Since the U.S. would have a much higher price differential, let's be more realistic than the HHS and assume about 20 percent usage in the U.S.

The math, then, is quite simple. We would save 40 percent of the drug cost on 20 percent of the market, which would result in an 8 percent savings (*not* 1 or 2 percent). Our drug spending is more than $200 billion, so this would result in savings of more than $16 billion.

No wonder the drug companies were nervous. The HHS report was so misleading that I wrote a third op-ed about this situation, published in New Jersey's *Star-Ledger*.

The Disappearing Bonus

I thought that eventually the articles and the journalists who kept calling would stop, but they didn't—it all continued, with new speeches and new radio shows, week after week, month after month. During this time, I didn't hear a word from Pfizer. How long would they continue to pay me and sit back without doing anything further? I didn't have to wait more than a couple of months to find out. On February 18, 2005, I received an e-mail from Pfizer's HR department that said, "The Annual Incentive Plan (AIP) is one of a number of compensation programs that Pfizer offers to support pay for performance. 2004 AIP awards will be distributed on March 11, 2005, for eligible colleagues."

I waited and waited, but nothing happened. For the first time in my recent career I didn't receive any bonus. When a few weeks had passed by I called the Justice Department in New Jersey, as I had been requested to do if Pfizer took any additional retaliatory action against me. And so it came about that I again met with James Nobile, chief of the special prosecutions division, and agent Stanley Beet.

In spite of the fact that I had been down to Washington, DC, only a month earlier for a formal testimony before the Senate Health, Education, Labor and Pensions committee, Jim didn't think that the law against dissuading someone from appearing before congress would help my case. Instead, he focused on retaliation—interfering with my livelihood, for providing a law enforcement officer information relating to the possible commission of a federal offense, in accordance with title 18 U.S.C. §1513(e). And this time he wanted to know who at the SEC as well as other law enforcement agencies I had talked to.

Pfizer's Second Letter to Congress

Meanwhile Pfizer had started to take a slightly different approach. When they found out that I was going to testify before Senator Kennedy and a few other well known names in the Senate, they wrote a second letter to congress. But this time the letter had a very different tone than the first one. They acknowledged up front that, "while any citizen is entitled to speak before the Congress, Dr. Rost is not speaking on behalf of Pfizer." They had finally admitted that what I was doing *was* legal and my right as a U.S. citizen. But they added a new twist: "It has been a number of years since Dr. Rost was stationed in Europe and we believe that his knowledge is outdated." Then Pfizer claimed that it was incorrect to suggest that consumers in Europe saved money on parallel-traded drugs. They used a study by the London School of Economics, which claimed that national health systems within the EU realized minimal savings from parallel-traded products. This was the same study the HHS report had based *their* conclusion upon.

There was just one thing both the HHS report and the Pfizer letter forgot to mention. This "study" had been funded by the drug industry.

TWENTY-FOUR

The "Disenabled" E-Mail Account

ON JUNE 5, 2005, CBS FINALLY BROADCAST the *60 Minutes* episode on drug reimportation that they had spent over six months producing. My biggest surprise, once I viewed it, was how much work had gone into it. Television, as I had experienced it, resembled a conveyor belt, on which guests were rolled into the studio for five minutes of live questioning and then rolled out again. But with *60 Minutes*, even the brief bits that featured me involved a tremendous amount of effort. They had come to my home twice, and they had followed me everywhere, from my speech to Vermont lawmakers to Washington, where they taped my testimony before Senator Kennedy and Senator Enzi. My family even got to see the personal side of Bob Simon, who spent the time between tapings in my house chasing my three-year-old around.

The *60 Minutes* broadcast worked out beautifully. Not only did I get a wider audience for my message on drug importation, but they had also been able to interview Dr. Richard Carmona, the U.S. Surgeon General, who admitted that reimportation could be done safely. The pharmaceutical industry association PhARMA refused to participate, afraid of how they would come across. The pivotal moment during the *60 Minutes* show came after Bob Simon asked me how many cases of death or serious diseases there had been due to reimportation. I told him, "There have been none known due to this practice."[1] He asked a similar question to Pfizer's unsuspecting VP of Global Security: "Has anyone in Europe been hurt by taking a bad drug because of parallel trading?" Pfizer's security VP didn't see the trap coming and responded, as on cue, "I don't know that anyone has, but the point is that we're making the safety issue before that happens."[2]

Wham! The door closed down behind him and he and every opponent of reimportation was caught in their own web of misinformation. In one moment of truth, the person who was responsible for fighting reimportation within Pfizer, who had made the argument over and over again that safety was his main concern, admitted on public television that he didn't know of a single individual in Europe who had been hurt by reimported drugs, in spite of this taking place for over twenty years.

Finally, they topped the show off with Senator Kennedy asking me, "Dr. Rost, do you still work for Pfizer?" to a round of laughter. What few knew was that this was a planted question, something I had asked him to ask me. My idea was that this would give me the opportunity to talk about legal protection for political activity; however, he posed the question with such aplomb and incredulity that it immediately became one of the most quoted comments from the Senate HELP committee hearing on drug importation.

It was simply a beautiful television moment that said it all. The fact that *60 Minutes* is one of the most widely viewed news shows, seen by an estimated 16 million viewers, ensured the message got out. Unfortunately, however, there was no significant mention of the CBS reimportation segment in the print media, and it might have remained that way had Pfizer not made yet another mistake.

"Your E-Mail Has Been Disenabled"

On Monday evening, the day after the broadcast, I sat down at my company computer to download my e-mail and find out if there were any comments from Pfizer colleagues about the show. Access to my e-mail account was immediately denied, but since Pfizer's IT department had helped me with the same problem three weeks earlier, I wasn't too worried and simply picked up the phone and called for help. The technician who responded initially told me there was a password issue. Then the line went silent for what seemed like a very long minute. When he came back on the phone again, he sounded serious.

"Your e-mail account has been disenabled. I can't start it again."

"What do you mean disenabled? Why has this happened?"

"I don't know; you'll have to contact your supervisor."

I asked him a few more questions but didn't get anywhere with him. And I figured it wouldn't help if I told the man that, in fact, I didn't know who my supervisor was.

I had been officially shut down. To make matters worse, I had also just discovered that Pfizer had turned off my cell phone. They had recently sent me an e-mail telling me that my phone might be turned off if I didn't move the billing from a central account to my corporate American Express card. There was only one problem with these instructions. I had been notified by American Express that Pfizer had also cancelled my credit card.

New Contact Information

As I had in the past, I decided to turn my rapidly deteriorating employment situation to my advantage. I had been very careful not to say anything about Pfizer's business in my public speeches or talk about what was going on internally, but clearly it couldn't be against any Pfizer policy to inform my friends and business contacts that my corporate e-mail and cell phone no longer worked.

So I wrote a short e-mail with my new contact information. I told them, "Pfizer just disconnected my cell phone and disabled access to my corporate e-mail account." I also added that, "I'm not that worried though. My office phone is still working. And Pfizer is committed to treating all employees with honesty, fairness, and respect. They strive to uphold the personal dignity of each individual and honor diversity, according to Pfizer's Policy on Business Conduct."

I couldn't help being a bit sarcastic and ended the mail, "I also know they embrace our political system with one vote for every corporation, oops, I meant individual. So, of course they embrace political diversity among employees. After all, they'd look bad if they didn't support democracy, free speech, and a citizen's right to appear before Congress, wouldn't they? They just don't want me to work so hard anymore. Things could be worse—I could be working weekends."

What I didn't expect was the reaction I got. The *New York Times* even sent over a photographer to take new pictures. I have to admit that I was pretty surprised, but I tried to answer their questions as comprehensively as possible, including the fact that I hadn't accessed my e-mail for almost two weeks, so I didn't know exactly when Pfizer had disenabled my system. (This led Bloomberg News to cancel their story.) I also called Pfizer's IT department, and the technician told me that the log didn't show what date my e-mail had been disenabled.

Over at Pfizer's PR department the phone calls from the press clearly took them by complete surprise. Initially they refused to reply and *Brandweek* wrote, "Pfizer did not return a call at press time."[3] After a while, however, they got their act together, which caused *Brandweek* to do an update in which they wrote, "Confusion reigned at Pfizer on Tuesday over the status of Peter Rost, the drug giant's VP-marketing for endocrine drugs."[4]

Telling the Press about My Situation

I didn't feel it made sense to try to protect Pfizer by not commenting on my employment status; clearly the shutdown of phone and e-mail made it impossible not to discuss these things. So for the first time, I informed the press that Pfizer had also taken away all work from me, and that I didn't even know the name of my supervisor.

This led Alex Berenson of the *New York Times* to write, "No man is an island. But Peter Rost is getting close."[5] Berenson continued: "First, his employees stopped reporting to him. Then his supervisors stopped returning his calls and now he does not know whom to report to. His secretary left, he said, and he was moved to an office near Pfizer's security department at a company building in Peapack, N.J. The latest blow came Monday, the morning after Dr. Rost, 46, appeared on a segment of *60 Minutes* on CBS about drug prices—a follow-up to his news conference on the subject last year with members of Congress and to the opinion pieces he has written for the *New York Times* and other newspapers. Ready, as always, to put in a full day at the office, Dr. Rost turned on his computer Monday and tried for the first time in almost two weeks to log into his Pfizer e-mail account. Access denied."

A spokesman for Pfizer told the *New York Times* that the company had not deliberately disconnected my e-mail and cell phone service. He said, "There have been cases, through a change of vendor, where some employees have lost service for a period of time." The Associated Press (AP) reported that "numerous company employees had suffered cell phone service problems recently." Pfizer's PR department explained that Pfizer "was requiring some people to create more e-mail passwords, causing some disruptions." The AP also tried to find out about the situation with my lack of a supervisor; however, Pfizer wouldn't comment on that.[6]

But it was too late for Pfizer's damage control. The press smelled blood in the water and Berenson wrote, "Dr. Rost may have additional protection against being fired. In its most recent annual report, Pfizer disclosed that the Justice Department had opened an investigation into its marketing of Genotropin, the growth hormone Dr. Rost was responsible for selling at Pharmacia. Dr. Rost said he could not confirm or deny whether he was involved in that investigation. But if he is, he may be protected by federal laws shielding whistle-blowers from retaliation."[7]

Alex Berenson ended the article writing, "Dr. Rost said that he did not enjoy being unable to work productively, but that he could not quit without another job to replace his current annual compensation of more than $600,000. 'I have a family to support. There haven't been that many job offers coming through lately.'"

My Salary

My wife, who is a very private individual, was absolutely furious that I had disclosed my salary information. Pharmacia had been paying very well, and my performance had resulted in even higher pay. I knew that Pfizer didn't like to pay their own people more than they absolutely had to, so perhaps, I thought, this information would be helpful to some of my Pfizer colleagues as they negotiated their next raise.

I didn't have to wait long for the public reaction to this information. On the message board *Café Pharma*, created for pharmaceutical sales reps, comments on Pfizer's board ranged from, "The guys got a set of brass balls. I'll give him that . . ." to "He's awesome—finally one person who will tell Hank to stick it," and "He's a self promoter. All his statements are for the greater glory of himself." Yet another wrote, "This guy is a disgrace, he doesn't get paid to do the stuff he's doing. If reps aren't allowed to speak to the media on issues, why should this dork."

The fact that I had a competitive salary also didn't pass unnoticed. Someone wrote, "I would love to see this guy justify a $600k salary. What could he possibly have done to be worth this?" Another employee responded, "When Dr. Rost finds another position, Hank will be $600K closer to his target $4bn in cuts."

Others didn't hold my salary against me, "I agree that top executives are WAY overpaid. On the other hand, this guy is risking that 600K, and I assume he believes absolutely in what he is saying. Would you risk your job to fight a practice or behavior within your company that you believed was wrong?"

Since I really didn't have much to do at work, I enjoyed every moment when I could interact with the outside world. In that sense, talking to the newspapers was actually a way to stay mentally alert during a period when my isolation would otherwise have driven me crazy. It wasn't a matter of doing something "for the greater glory of himself," as one colleague had put it, but to keep my mind alive and avoid being carried away by men dressed in white coats after two years of doing virtually nothing at work; living in the corporate twilight zone.

Pfizer Blinks

I decided to rattle Pfizer's cage a bit more. First I wrote an e-mail to Pfizer's IT director. I asked, "How come the IT department yesterday evening refused to restore my account and instructed me to talk to my supervisor, if this was an automatic routine event, and today when the newspapers called it was fixed right away? How do I deal with problems in the future when Pfizer refuses to tell me who my supervisor is?"[8]

Pfizer had worked too hard to try to make my e-mail and cell phone problems appear as normal events, I wondered how they would feel about me revealing that these were the least of my problems, that I was much more concerned about the fact that they had just cut my compensation in half, by deleting my annual bonus, and taken away my annual stock-option allocation. I had no illusions that Pfizer would suddenly change their mind, but it would be instructive to see how they responded. So I also wrote an e-mail on my newly restored account and sent it to Pfizer's PR department and to Ronald Chapman. Ronald had recently been promoted to Pfizer's Vice Chairman and General Counsel. I thanked Pfizer for their assistance in getting my e-mail and cell phone working and I expressed my sadness that so many people had experienced similar problems. I only hoped that Pfizer's IT department had assisted them when they called for help and hadn't refused to connect them the way they refused to re-enable my e-mail account when I called for assistance. I thought I should make sure that my missing bonus and stock options were not another glitch. So, I politely suggested I would give them until the end of the week to confirm that it wasn't another "mistake" that Pfizer had withheld my bonus and stock options.[9]

What Pfizer didn't know was that I had equipped both these e-mails with an electronic tracer, so that I could see each time they opened my e-mails and who else they forwarded them to. I knew that this wouldn't be something that impacted my legal situation; however,

I was isolated and I knew that my little game would provide days of entertainment as I followed the reaction within Pfizer. Also, Pfizer had always reserved the right to spy on any employee's corporate e-mail messages so I was delighted that I could, in a small way, return the attention.

Spying On the Spymasters

It didn't take long for my computer screen to light up like a Fourth-of-July celebration. My two messages bounced back and forth within Pfizer, then hit the law firm Partland & Longhorn in Washington, then Partland & Longhorn in New York. Within a few days, the messages had been opened over 100 times. It then suddenly appeared on an entirely new ISP, owned by an organization called "WPP Group U.S. Investments Inc"—one of the world's largest communications services groups. Their PR companies include a dozen firms, among them Burson-Marsteller and Hill & Knowlton in New York. I couldn't know which one of these PR firms was studying my question about my compensation, but now I knew that I was up against not just the largest pharmaceutical company in the world and the best lawyers money could buy, but also the best PR machine ever invented.

For a moment I wondered if I had gone too far, but that feeling soon passed, replaced by glee as I also discovered that my message made its way to the New Jersey branch of Epstein, Becker & Green, a law firm with one of the largest labor and employment practices worldwide, and to Dickstein, Shapiro, Morin & Oshinsky. I was impressed: One guy asks about his missing bonus and three world-class law firms and one global public relations and advertising conglomerate get involved. It was clear that I was outgunned; but perhaps Pfizer had finally started taking me seriously.

I guessed by the number of times my message was opened by all these people that they were working feverishly on a reply. And I wasn't disappointed. Pfizer was very careful to respond within my deadline, which again indicated that they were truly worried about what I might do. On the day I had requested a response, my lawyer received a three-page letter from Stewart Bolling of Partland & Longhorn.[10]

Another Furious Pfizer Letter

It was an unusual letter, not just because of the hostile tone, but also because of the many statements Pfizer claimed I had made that I didn't recognize. In fact the only statement I agreed with was the one where they truthfully wrote that I hadn't done much work. "The decision not to award a bonus recognizes the reality, which I believe even your client would not dispute, that he has not done any work of significance for Pfizer in the past year or contributed to the business." There was, indeed, virtually nothing else in the letter that I agreed with.

In my e-mail I had asked Ronald "to confirm that Pfizer has deliberately withheld my bonus and stock options, which effectively cuts my compensation in half." In response, Bolling stated that "for at least the past year Dr. Rost has not had any functional responsibilities whatsoever." He also wrote that "the decision not to award Dr. Rost a bonus was entirely appropriate and made long before his appearance on *60 Minutes* was aired." Bolling also wrote that I had been "threatening Pfizer personnel with damaging publicity," The letter stated that "Dr. Rost made an explicit threat that he would again go to the media to embarrass Pfizer if Pfizer did not agree to pay him a 'substantial' bonus by this Friday, June 17." Of course I hadn't made such a threat, but clearly the fact that I asked for my bonus in connection with talking about how a congressman might help me really scared Pfizer, which was the objective.

Bolling also claimed that "Dr. Rost made it clear that he would only accept a position at VP level or above," even though I never had made such a request. I was also surprised about the reference to "Dr. Rost's threats to embarrass and defame the company." If I make truthful statements about my employment and compensation, I am not defaming Pfizer; no matter how embarrassing Pfizer's decisions may appear to the company.

The letter did leave me with the impression that Pfizer was, indeed, so embarrassed by their own acts that perhaps they would consider the consequences of such decisions more carefully in the future. But the action didn't stop with this letter. On the spur of the moment, I had also written to Pfizer's IT director in my first e-mail and told him, "Perhaps you can link back to the internal lawyers who are dealing with all this and ask them to identify themselves, as well as my formal supervisor." I also wrote, "It's ridiculous to be informed by a journalist, that I still have my job and I can't see how it is in Pfizer's best interest to behave in this manner." I knew he'd immediately forward this to whomever was in charge of the "Peter Rost case."

A few weeks later I received an e-mail from a Human Resources person who told me that she would be my day-to-day contact, that my responsibilities for the endocrine care area ended in 2003, and that I had been retained solely to cooperate with the legal department at Pfizer. She also wrote that I had no ongoing business responsibilities and that there was no need for me to communicate with anyone on the business side of the company.[11]

I couldn't help but note how these statements completely contradicted what Pfizer told the *New York Times* on June 8, 2005. While they had refused to comment on my work, they claimed that Pfizer had not changed my responsibilities since April 2003, when Pfizer bought Pharmacia.[12] The truth was that in April 2003 I was still in charge of my entire department, and now I had nothing.

TWENTY-FIVE

Admissions by Pfizer's CEO

RECALLING HOW EFFECTIVE MY review of Marcia Angell's book on Amazon.com had been, the April 2005 publication of Pfizer CEO Hank McKinnell's book *A Call to Action*— a book about the pharma industry and healthcare policy—gave me an opportunity to create more chaos. Tendentious and boring as I expected this book would be, I soon realized that, in fact, it was filled with so many amazing statements that I decided not just to do a review on Amazon, but to also distribute the review through a press release distributed to all news media and on the net.

MEA CULPA BY A BIG PHARMA CEO, July 5, 2005

Pfizer's CEO, Dr. Hank McKinnell has written an astonishing book in which he admits that he doesn't always believe in what he's saying [11], that drugs from Canadian pharmacies are safe [69] and that high U.S. drug prices have nothing to do with past R&D expenses [46]. He also writes that "perhaps pharmaceuticals represent too low a percentage of total healthcare spending" [45] and he calls for "price controls to be lifted" around the world [64], because "It is time for Canadians and others to pay their fair share." [65]. He also calls for a doubling of drug patent life [185] which would result in a drastic reduction of new, low-priced generic drugs.

Dr. McKinnell starts his book with the surprising confession that he doesn't always believe in what he's saying. "They listened to my logic, but I could tell they weren't convinced, and to tell you the truth, I wasn't either." [11]

He also doesn't shy away from embarrassing facts, "Branded drug prices are anywhere from 25-100 percent more expensive in the United States." [50] He even admits, "Drugs from Canadian pharmacies are as safe as drugs from pharmacies in the United States." [69]

But his impressive mea culpa doesn't stop there. He slams everyone who makes a connection between drug prices and R&D. "It's a fallacy to suggest that our industry, or any industry, prices a product to recapture the R&D budget spent in development." [46]

Finally, in an astonishing intellectual somersault, Dr. McKinnell claims that "price controls always make prices higher in the long run." [64] And since he wants to give people lower drug prices, by eliminating price controls, he writes, "Starting with pharmaceuticals, I call for price controls to be lifted in Canada and elsewhere." [64]

Dr. McKinnell ends his book with a wonderful quote by Gandhi, for those who desire change. "First they ignore you. Then they laugh at you. Then they fight you. Then you win." [193] Dr. McKinnell just doesn't realize that he has become "them."

In his book, Hank McKinnell wrote, "My motivation for writing this book isn't celebrity or fortune; all royalties are being donated to the Academic Alliance for Healthcare in Africa." It is hard to say what royalties the book was generating, but when I first viewed it, the book's Amazon.com sales rank was around 20,000—not terrible, but certainly not a bestseller. So it was with great satisfaction that I observed how, shortly after I had distributed my press release, the book jumped into the low thousands in ranking and stayed there for a month. More amazing, my press release was opened nearly 100,000 times.

An E-mail from Hank McKinnell's Ghost Writer

But something much more amazing happened after I sent out the press release; John Kador, Hank McKinnell's ghost writer or co-author, wrote a revealing e-mail to me, which was so remarkable that I decided to forward it to some of the newspapers. In his e-mail Mr. Kador told me that he had assisted Hank in putting *A Call to Action* together and that he appreciated my close reading of the book. He also wrote that he had wanted to contact me when they were writing the book, because he felt that my position on drug reimportation was more correct than Pfizer's official opposition on safety.

This sensational e-mail caused Jim Edwards to pen the headline "Pfizer Fable takes Another Strange Twist," in a *Brandweek* article. He wrote, "The e-mail is a publicity coup for Rost because it suggests that the Pfizer chief's own writer thinks the company's position on reimportation is a loser."[1]

And under the headline "Another stinger from Pfizer's gadfly," Ed Silverman from the New Jersey *Star-Ledger* wrote that now I had found another way to annoy Pfizer. He went on to describe my Amazon.com review of *A Call to Action* and the fact that McKinnell wrote that he didn't always believe in what he was saying.[2] Then Ed quoted Kador's e-mail to me in which he had written, "I actually wanted to contact you when we were writing this book, because I felt your position on drug reimportation was more correct than Pfizer's official opposition on safety." Kador went so far as to state, "I think Hank's thinking (and this is a personal book) can diverge from official Pfizer positions."[3]

TWENTY-SIX

Fighting a War

THERE ARE TWO WAYS TO DO PUBLIC RELATIONS—the way the big drug companies do it, or the way I have done it—and I want to explain how this works, and how I was able to get so much publicity that Pfizer's lawyers repeatedly asked me which PR agency I worked with.

Let's first look at the drug companies. When they do public relations, they don't do it themselves. They hire global PR firms that charge $500 an hour for their services. At these firms work some of the finest communications specialists, former journalists, and news anchors. The purpose of public relations, as opposed to advertising, is for the public *not* to realize that they are listening to a commercial message. This is what makes a deft public relations campaign so effective.

It can be done many different ways. The most obvious ones are to send out a press release with information about an issue to newspapers and other media and hope they pick it up. Another way is to film a video news release, make it look like a news segment, and have it transmitted to all the television stations around the country. Many of these stations are strapped for cash and are willing to play these disguised commercials; some even go so far as to add their own voice-over or have one of their journalists read the scripts. And the public never knows.[1]

Another insidious—and effective—way to do public relations is to support others to act as your "front persons." The pharmaceutical industry has done a great job in supporting various "patient advocacy groups," and once they are beholden to the industry these organizations do the industry's bidding. If the patient organization for a particular area doesn't play along, this is easy to overcome—simply set up a fake competing organization, start getting new members, and *voila*, there is someone who can get the message out without journalists suspecting a thing. "I don't think there is a patient-advocacy group in America that does not receive some level of funding from a pharmaceutical company," said Nancy Davenport-Ennis, head of the National Patient Advocate Foundation to Jim Drinkard of *USA Today*.[2]

USA Today also wrote that the drug industry has "1,274 lobbyists—more than two for every member of Congress." Sen. Chuck Grassley, (R-Iowa), chairman of the Senate Finance Committee, was quoted saying, "They are powerful. You can hardly swing a cat by the tail in that town without hitting a pharmaceutical lobbyist."

How to Manipulate American Consumers

There are very few entities that can counter-balance all this money. Probably the most powerful opponent is the news media itself, though not even they are always up to the challenge. This is especially true for some medical journals. There is a bottom rung that will accept any paper or any study or any write-up done by a for-hire "medical-education agency." The drug company or the agency then pays an opinion leader to put his name on the paper.

In fact, this doesn't just happen with the low level journals. Alex Berenson from the *New York Times* in 2005 wrote an article about a contentious Vioxx study which included a potentially mislabeled patient. According to the *Times*, Dr. Jeffrey R. Lisse, a rheumatologist at the University of Arizona, who was listed as the study's first author, said that Merck actually wrote the report.[3] The report appeared in *Annals of Internal Medicine*, a top-of-the line journal—that purports to adhere to the highest standards. The public at large has no way of knowing this, nor do many doctors, just like they don't know when a pharmaceutical company has paid a celebrity spokesperson to talk about their disease or their drug on a television news show.

In reality, the American consumer is already completely manipulated by these schemes that go on below the surface. The drug industry is no different from many other companies, and they do what they can to support laws that will benefit them, not the consumers. One of the most amazing examples of this was when congress passed the Medicare drug bill, which gave prescription drug coverage to seniors, starting in 2006, but only covered $1,000 of the first $5,000 expense, and also explicitly forbade the government from negotiating drug prices.[4] To make matters even worse, the *Los Angeles Times* revealed that Costco's prices on the top one hundred drugs used by Medicare beat prices of all forty-eight plans in California in more than half the cases.[5]

The manipulation encompasses every part of society, from scientists at the renowned National Institutes of Health (NIH) taking drug company money, to other government agencies, such as the FDA, which gets a large part of their funding directly from the drug industry. So when drug companies sponsor medical opinion leaders to do speeches, when they send them out on trips across the country, or give grants for their research or to their universities, no one should believe that this is done out of charity. It is done for one reason, and that is to sell more drugs. Look at the money trail and you will understand who is in control.

Taking On the Dragon

So how, then, can one person stand up to this formidable environment? About the only protection a person has is public opinion and the news media. It is not a big deal for a corporation to break the law and a few years later settle an employment conflict and pay out dimes on the dollar. If there is anything a big corporation has a lot of, it is money, whether they deal with tiny employment suits or large government investigations. And even $100 million fines virtually never affect the share price, so shareholders couldn't care less. In fact, because of the uncertainty a large legal proceeding entails, after paying a fine the company share price often increases. But it is a big deal to lose face. Very rarely do we hear companies admitting any guilt for anything. The most common corporate statement after a legal settlement with a regulatory or a law enforcement agency is "the company neither admits nor denies the charges."

So a single individual can win if he allies himself with the press or with law enforcement. Obviously, "winning" is a matter of definition. That individual may never work in the same industry again, nor may he *ever* get same kind of income, but he may win in the eyes of the public opinion.

The reason my story was of interest was because I could offer something priceless: a personal sacrifice. If my attorney had told me it was a wonderful idea to start speaking out in favor of drug importation, and if my employer had sent roses to me, no one would have been interested in my story. But because I broke ranks, because I was a senior executive with an understanding of the inner workings of my industry, who spoke in opposition to my employer—with everything to lose and a very little to gain (it's not like anyone paid me to appear or I received new job offers)—I was able to create news. It is not something that I, or anyone, can easily repeat or would want to repeat, because the basis for that news is your own personal career and future. What helped me do this is my belief that I am convinced anything is possible.

As President Calvin Coolidge said, "Nothing in the world can take the place of persistence; talent will not, nothing is more common than unsuccessful men with talent; genius will not; unrewarded genius just say is almost a proverb; education will not; the world is full of educated derelicts. Persistence and determination alone are omnipotent."

What *is* important is to take action.

I didn't always think this way. I didn't want to become a whistle-blower. I didn't want to write this book. But in the end, I had to; I just couldn't let the crooks win. The fact that you have just read this book means—to me—that I *have* won my fight against an overpowering opponent.

But of course, the story doesn't end here. Just when I finished writing this manuscript, I got a call from the Justice Department's criminal division. A few days later I met with an FBI agent and the Deputy Health Care Fraud Chief in Boston.

And that is when I realized that it will take a long time until this story ends. This book is just the beginning of an amazing journey, so different from anything I could've imagined. It is not a voyage I knew I would chose a few years back, or that I could ever have imagined that I would take. So I will just try to enjoy, and make the most of every day. Because it isn't the final destination that matters, it is the pleasure you take from traveling to it.

Afterword

PFIZER FIRED ME on December 1, 2005.

I was informed of my termination by journalists, not by Pfizer. I was in Costa Rica, lecturing on reimportation of drugs. This was a meeting well publicized in advance and I couldn't help but feel faintly flattered that Pfizer had waited until I was out of the country to let the ax fall. When I returned home I discovered my termination letter taped to my front door. The person who brought the letter to my house had, apparently, had the foresight to also bring a tape roll.

For Pfizer my termination appeared to be a major event, celebrated by calling every major newspaper and offering interviews about this strategic corporate decision. They even called the producers at *60 Minutes*, hoping, that perhaps this would merit yet another segment. In doing so, they may have miscalculated. Instead of doing a show about my humbling termination, *60 Minutes* called me and asked me to participate in a new story about the anti-aging industry.

Pfizer didn't simply terminate my employment—in a carefully orchestrated media strategy they also made the titillating public revelation that I'd filed a *qui tam* lawsuit against the company. The False Claims Act allows private individuals to sue in the name of the U.S. government when the government has lost money based on sales, marketing, and other practices that violate federal laws. The person who files the suit can also collect a substantial share of any fines, which sometimes run into the hundreds of millions.

My lawsuit, filed back in 2003, alleged that, from about 1997 until 2003, Pharmacia illegally promoted Genotropin for off-label uses for anti-aging in adults and short-stature in children unrelated to growth hormone deficiency. I had not been allowed to talk about the suit, much less write a word in this book, since it had been filed under seal. The Justice Department in November 2005 declined to intervene in this civil action, leading the court to unseal the suit. The bad part about this development is that my lawyers will now have to do all the legal work on their own. The good news is that my minimum share of any fine has almost doubled, from 15 percent to 25 percent.

Pfizer, however, didn't just reveal my *qui tam* action to the media; they also submitted a motion to have the case dismissed, which they released to the press. In addition, the company tried to convince journalists that the fact that the Justice Department hadn't intervened meant that my suit was without merit. Many journalists did their own fact checking, and Bloomberg News interviewed Patrick Burns, Director of Communications for the Taxpayers Against Fraud Education Fund. This is a non-profit organization in Washington, DC, which assists whistleblowers and their attorneys. Mr. Burns is quoted saying, "The fact the Justice Department won't join the suit doesn't mean the end of Rost's case. The Department of Justice simply does not have enough lawyers and investigators to handle the volume of false claims act suits coming its way. There are right now 150 cases under seal and under investigation, covering more than 500 drugs."[1]

This sentiment was echoed in another interview in *Macleans*, a Canadian weekly newsmagazine, in which Danylo Hawaleshka quoted Kenneth Nolan, a Florida-based authority on whistleblower suits, who said that just because the government declines a case does not mean it isn't worth pursuing. "There are plenty of meritorious cases that are declined each year," he said. In fact, Nolan also claimed that U.S. authorities often lack the resources to pursue a *qui tam*, and prefer to let private citizens do the legal legwork.[2]

From certain documents Pfizer attached to their "motion to dismiss," I learned that, after many of my coworkers and I had helped Pfizer address the problems in the Genotropin franchise, Pfizer had turned around and tried to paint us all—the people who tried to clean up—as crooks: In a May 19, 2003, letter to the FDA about the Genotropin "corrective measures" Pfizer took, the corporation wrote, "Pfizer has replaced or is in the process of replacing senior sales and marketing personnel in the Genotropin product line and disciplining certain sales representatives. Indeed, due to the merger, Pfizer has placed entirely new senior management in charge of the Genotropin product line."

Additionally, in a June 3, 2003, letter to the Office of the Inspector General, HHS, Pfizer wrote, "Pfizer has taken a number of steps to address these issues, including the appointment of new senior management responsible for the marketing and distribution of Genotropin." Not a word that I had been pushing them for months to take action and that in response to this they'd threatened to fire me.

Pfizer's attempt at character assassination didn't stop there. The American Council on Science and Health on December 30, 2005, announced that they had nominated me to "Whiny Whistleblower of the Year." In his nomination, Gilbert Ross, M.D., Executive and Medical Director of the ACSH, stated that the biggest "Whiny Whistleblower" for 2005 was "the person who most outrageously defied his or her employer, regardless of loyalty, science, or even common sense." Dr. Ross wrote, "I vote for ex-Pfizer V.P. Dr. Peter Rost, an inept exec but a pretty good whistleblower. He provoked a federal investigation of his own company in 2003, alleging that Pfizer was responsible for the improper marketing of the synthetic growth hormone Genotropin."[3]

According to the "Center for Science in the Public Interest" (www.cspinet.org) the following drug companies had at one time or another contributed to ACSH: Pfizer, Bristol-Myers Squibb, Merck, Abbott Laboratories, Eli Lilly, American Cyanamid, Ciba-Geigy, Hoffman-La Roche, Johnson & Johnson, Rhone-Poulenc, Sandoz, Searle, Syntex, Warner-Lambert, Upjohn, and the Pharmaceutical Manufacturers Association.[4]

In a way I felt honored to be officially nominated 'Whiny Whistleblower of the Year' by a front organization paid by Pfizer and Big Pharma, since I apparently competed against two real consumer heroes; Dr. David Graham, FDA, and Dr. Eric Topol, the Cleveland Clinic.

What was most revealing about this episode is that according to the magazine *Mother Jones*, "Ross spent all of 1996 at a federal prison camp in Schuylkill, Pennsylvania, having being sentenced to forty-six months in prison for his participation in a scheme that ultimately defrauded New York's Medicaid program of approximately $8 million."[5]

The drama also mounted behind the scenes. The *qui tam* team at my law firm had moved to a new firm which had a potential conflict of interest. So I was forced to find a new firm to take on my case and if I failed to do so the suit would be lost, since I wouldn't have an advocate that could oppose Pfizer's motion. Fortunately, the case was perceived to be so good that several law firms expressed interest and I was able to sign on with one of the best litigation firms in New York.

But my *qui tam* complaint hadn't only resulted in a civil investigation; because of the law that makes it a criminal offense to knowingly distribute growth hormone for off-label usage, the Justice Department's criminal division, in the summer of 2005, also started an investigation.

I had, in fact, been a witness and testified twice before a grand jury during the fall of 2005. The Fifth Amendment to the U.S. Constitution requires that charges for all capital and "infamous" crimes be brought by an indictment returned by a grand jury. The grand jury is responsible for deciding whether there is sufficient evidence to indict a defendant. Based on the questions I received during my testimony, the prosecutor wanted to know if Pfizer had been forced to come forward or if they had truly reported what I told them "voluntarily." The questions also indicated that the Justice Department was very interested in learning for how long the potential illegal activities had continued after Pfizer took over Pharmacia.

I have to admit that I was surprised that Pfizer terminated my employment right in the middle of this criminal investigation. In their eagerness to get rid of me, Pfizer not only embarrassed the United States Attorney's Office by terminating a federal grand jury witness in an ongoing investigation, but also showed blatant disrespect for U.S. Congress and the Congressmen who on September 30, 2004, sent an open letter to Pfizer's CEO and Board of Directors, stating, "We are writing to express our serious concerns at the intimidation being directed at Pfizer Vice President Peter Rost."[6]

I ought also to give Pfizer's side of the story. In their termination letter they wrote, "We maintained your employment over the past two years to avoid any complications that might have arisen from a severance or other employment-related action, particularly in light of the fact that the government was reviewing claims that you had raised."[7]

Pfizer allegedly also has a history of firing whistleblowers. The *Wall Street Journal* has described how Dr. Juan Walterspiel was fired when he raised ethical issues.[8] Expressing an opinion that certain conduct is illegal is protected by the New Jersey Conscientious Employee Protection Act. An employer who retaliates against an employee who engages in protected conduct violates this statute.

Based on this, the law firm of Green & Savits filed a wrongful termination lawsuit against Pfizer, Inc., Hank McKinnell, and other senior officers on December 12, 2005. (A copy of my complaint and supporting documents can be viewed on Green & Savits website: http://www.greensavits.com/rostvpfizer.shtml.) The complaint alleges that Pfizer violated the New Jersey Conscientious Employee Protection Act, the whistle-blowing prohibition of the False Claims Act, New Jersey common law public policy prohibiting retaliation against whistleblowers, and retaliated against a grand jury witness in violation of federal law.

There is no question in my mind that Pfizer's termination of whistleblowers sends chilling signals to honest employees within the company. The media campaign they unleashed when they fired me served the same purpose. Pfizer's outrage was apparent. A Pfizer spokesperson was quoted in the *New York Times* on December 2, 2005, saying, "He was essentially blowing the whistle on his own conduct," and that my actions in filing a *qui tam* complaint "were clearly opportunistic."[9] They appeared to have forgotten all about the May 28, 2003, letter from Pfizer's general counsel, in which Mr. Kindler admitted that I was the one who made Pfizer aware of the Genotropin legal issues. He also wrote, "I recognize, that with your assistance, Pharmacia examined these issues in 2002," and he validated my concerns that Pharmacia had not taken appropriate action by saying that Pfizer would contact the government and make "additional changes."

I received this letter a week after I filed my *qui tam* complaint, but the date on the letter makes it look as if I should have received the letter well before. This was the subject of detailed questioning during my grand jury testimony. I was only too happy to provide the Justice Department with an e-mail I wrote to Pfizer to confirm the actual date I received the letter.[10]

Perhaps Pfizer's elaborate attempt to discredit an employee who tried to clean up illegal conduct which started years before his own employment should not be surprising, considering that Pfizer has the unusual dishonor of having been forced to sign not just one but two corporate integrity agreements[11] with the HHS Office of the Inspector General and paid close to half a billion dollars in criminal and civil fines.[12] According to the Department of Justice, Pfizer's $240 million criminal fine for Neurontin was "the second largest criminal fine ever imposed in a health care fraud prosecution." The same team at the Justice Department in Boston who declined intervention in the Neurontin case, which generated a total of $430 million in criminal and civil fines, also declined intervention in the Genotropin case.

So why did I start all of this? Why did I ever file the *qui tam* lawsuit against Pfizer that resulted in this ruckus? Let me give you some background on what I couldn't write about until now, without violating the seal of the complaint. At the end of Pharmacia's internal investigation in 2002 it was my understanding that Pharmacia didn't contact the government, which would have been appropriate. Because of my ongoing concerns, several colleagues and I informed Pfizer of certain legal issues in October and November 2002. I also detailed the legal exposure for Genotropin in an e-mail to Pfizer in January 2003. Pfizer's response was simple; they wrote that I would be fired.

Next I continued to try to force Pfizer to act, writing directly to Pfizer's general counsel. I ended the letter, "You have based on this e-mail at a minimum been able to make an informed decision not to take any action. Should this result in any future adverse events there is now a written record that the responsibility for this decision was placed at the appropriate level in the Pfizer management structure." In April 2003, right before my interrogation by Pfizer lawyers, I wrote Pfizer and told them they should inform the Justice Department about the issues we had discussed.

I perceived the questioning during that interrogation as hostile, and I was especially surprised by the last question Pfizer's lawyer asked me: Had I filed any suit or complaint against the company related to the Genotropin issues? He was clearly trying to find out if I had filed a *qui tam* suit, even though, as a lawyer, he should have known that such a suit would be filed under seal and couldn't be revealed. I answered no to that question, since I hadn't even retained *qui tam* counsel at that time. This line of questioning concerned me, and I decided that I could not afford for this situation not to be handled correctly—especially when distribution of growth hormone for off-label purposes is a felony. So I took action and filed my *qui tam* suit.

I really didn't have much choice once I had exhausted all internal avenues to get the company to take action. The reason for that is this is Title 18 U.S.C. §4, which states: "Whoever, having knowledge of the actual commission of a felony cognizable by a court of the United States, conceals and does not as soon as possible make known the same to some judge or other person in civil or military authority under the United States, shall be fined under this title or imprisoned not more than three years, or both."

None of us who became employed by Pharmacia asked to be put into an incriminating situation. The fact that the company didn't make sure we were protected, and instead made up to $50 million each year on off-label prescriptions, speaks for itself.

An employee faced with illegal corporate behavior has three choices. He can quit, join the conspiracy, or act. My choice was to act. Unfortunately, the end result is that I'm now unemployed for the first time in my life. And I'm not alone in that situation. The U.S. Department of Labor claims we have an unemployment rate of 4.9 percent.[13] According to *The Economist*, however, the true unemployment rate in the U.S. is over 8 percent, or 12.6 million Americans.[14] The difference is due to the fact that the U.S. government doesn't count people as unemployed after six months without a job.[15] And contrary to press reports, I have received no severance payments and for the first time in my life I am eligible for unemployment benefits of approximately $13,078.[16] At this annual income level my family of four would actually fall below the federal poverty level,[17] quite a difference from a year ago when my salary exceeded half a million dollars per year.[18]

I'm also uninsured for the first time in my life and I have to pay the full price for drugs, just like millions of other uninsured Americans. Contrary to many others, however, I do have a choice. In accordance with federal COBRA law, I was offered the opportunity to continue my health care coverage for eighteen months. There was only one hitch (with which many readers will be all too familiar); I had to pay $15,269 per year to receive this benefit.[19] I decided that with an income of $13,078, COBRA didn't make sense.

Clearly the system we have today isn't just broke. The system is utterly and completely sick and our weakest citizens are paying the price, every day. And while I have belatedly been forced to share some of the experiences of our poor, uninsured, and unemployed, my situation doesn't even start to compare with people with no resources, no voice, nowhere to go and no one to listen to them. For those citizens we have something that's called the government, a government that is supposed to look out for the people who can't look out for themselves, but instead focuses on "pay to play money."

Today's system is built on greed. Greed is defined as an excessive desire to acquire or possess more than someone needs or deserves. Greed is not a corporate executive who builds an organization such as Microsoft, creates a lot of jobs, and happens to get rich. Greed is to become CEO for a drug company such as Pfizer, be responsible for a stock price drop of close to 50 percent over a five-year tenure, twice as much as other companies in this industry,[20] secure a $83 million retirement package[21] while firing 16,385 Pharmacia and Pfizer employees,[22] and get a 72 percent pay increase to $16.6 million as his reward in 2004.[23]

According to the *New York Times*, average worker pay has remained flat since 1990, at around $27,000, after adjusting for inflation, while CEO compensation has quadrupled, from $2.82 million to $11.8 million.[24] Our CEOs are in a position in which they can basically use public companies as personal piggy banks. And this is perfectly legal as long as they get someone else to sign their check. Meanwhile, the federal minimum wage has remained at $5.15 an hour since September 1, 1997. In fact, after adjusting for inflation, the value of the minimum wage is at its second lowest level since 1955.[25]

At the same time, the pharmaceutical industry spends over $100 million on lobbying activities to stop lower drug prices, according to the Center for Public Integrity. There are 1,274 registered pharmaceutical lobbyists in Washington, DC. During the 2004 election cycle, the drug industry contributed $1 million to President Bush.[26] For an industry that makes $500 billion on a global basis, spending 1 million on a president or $100 million on lobbying is pocket change.[27]

This money was well spent. It stopped legalized import of cheaper drugs and bought the U.S. a new Medicare drug program. This $720 billion law includes $139 billion in profits to drug manufactures and

$46 billion in subsidies to HMOs and private insurance plans.[28] The program has been such a disaster for our poor; at least twenty-four states have been forced to enact emergency measures to ensure access to medications during the implementation of this law.[29] That's what a million dollars buys in Washington.

So how could this happen? The answer is simple. The American democracy has been stolen by our new class of robber barons—the CEOs of our largest corporations. A political system dependent on charity from rich men in hand-tailored suits with $100-million retirement packages is no democracy. It is a kleptocracy.[30] It is not what our founding fathers envisioned.

So, can we change this? *Can* we build a new future? I believe that we can. I believe this because we live in a country that could rid itself of slavery, a country that finally allowed women to vote; a country that has come a long way in the short time since the civil rights movement began. But early on, each of those incredible changes was fiercely opposed by those in power, and none took place without great sacrifice. To free our corporations from sticky-fingered CEOs, to free our elected representatives from "pay to play money," and to free our people from these tyrants is going to take sacrifice and time. Perhaps another one hundred years. In short, it will require a second American revolution. I believe that, one day, this will happen.

Peter Rost writes a daily blog on http://peterrost.blogspot.com/

Acknowledgments

I AM INDEBTED TO MANY PEOPLE IN THE LITERARY WORLD. First I salute my true star editor—Ed Stackler—who put the manuscript into readable shape and Rachael Crossland, who is more detail oriented than any editor I ever met. She checked every word and changed every paragraph.

I am also very grateful to the sixty-nine New York publishing editors who requested the book proposal and convinced me that this project really had a chance to succeed. Their gracious comments, claiming that the manuscript not only was "a zeitgeist book," "quite a page turner," "amazing," and "suspenseful," combined with comments that "it should be published as quickly as possible," convinced me to move forward.

I would also like to thank other professional writers who encouraged me to write this book. Alicia Mundy, the Washington correspondent for the *Seattle Times* and author of *Dispensing With the Truth: The Victims, the Drug Companies and the Dramatic Story Behind the Battle Behind Fen-Phen* was the first to tell me that I had to publish what I had experienced. Scott Hensley from *The Wall Street Journal* was the second person who asked me to write what really happened and the third was Jim Edwards from *Brandweek*. Marcia Angell, M.D., author of *The Truth About the Drug Companies: How They Deceive Us and What To Do About It*, helped me in ways only she could and so did former Pfizer sales rep Jamie Reidy, author of *Hard Sell: The Evolution of a Viagra Salesman*.

I am also deeply indebted to all the journalists who have covered my story. In particular, I would like to mention David Cay Johnston and Melody Peterson from the *New York Times*, who wrote the original Wyeth tax story; David Schwab and Ed Silverman at the New Jersey *Star-Ledger*, who never stopped asking probing questions; Theresa Agovino at Associated Press, who could crack an oyster open with her tough questions; Alex Berenson at the *New York Times*, who's writing is both witty and penetrating, and Robert Pear at the *New York Times* who's ability to extract key information is unparalleled.

I would also like to thank Maria Bartiromo and Mike Huckman from CNBC and their producer Bianna Golodryga. CNBC was the first television network to pick up on my message and they allowed me to keep coming back on their show. I also have to thank Bob Simon, Cathy Olian, and Frank Koughan from *60 Minutes*; they spent a long six months following me and taping my speeches. Finally, Chuck Hadad, together with Valerie Morris, from CNN did a great job of summarizing my story.

I also want to thank all the other journalists who have covered what I had to say; without them I could never have written this book. Names in order of article/broadcast appearance: Paul Beckett and Jathon Sapsford, *The Wall Street Journal*; Neil Cavuto, *Fox News*; Tim Craig, *Washington Post*; David Price, *Canadian Broadcasting Corporation*; Rita Rubin, *USA Today*; Klaus Marre, *The Hill*; Douglas Tallman, *The Gazette*; Aldo Santin, *Winnipeg Free Press*; Bill Theobald, *Indy Star*; Paul Adams, *Baltimore Sun*; Christopher Rowland, *Boston Globe*; Tony Pugh, *Knight-Ridder Newspapers*; Todd Zwillich, *WebMD*; Kristen Hallam and Nicole Ostrow, *Bloomberg News*; Matthew Kelly, *Hearst News Service*; Val Brickates Kennedy, CBS; Jo-Ann Moriarty, *Newhouse*; Julie Rovner and Emily Heil, *Congress Daily*; Eunice Khoury, *Well Preserved*; Jeff Cooperman, NBC; Sam Bishop *News-Miner*; Robert Bruss, *Bloomberg News*; Deborah Ray, *Healthy Talk Radio*; Jim Gransbery, *Billings Gazette*; Bob Anez, Associated Press; Tom Shine and Geoff Martz, ABC; John Lauerman, *Bloomberg News*; Jane Norman, *The Des Moines Register*; Danylo Hawaleshka and Leah Bowness, *Macleans*; Mary Beth

Schneider, *Indy Star*; Martin DeAgostino, *South Bend Tribune*; Mark Johnson, *Charlotte Observer*; Ann Potempa, *Anchorage Daily News*; Catherine Clabby, *News Observer*; Ruth Holladay, *Indy Star*; David Rice, *Winston-Salem Journal*; Hollister Hovey, *Dow Jones Newswires*; Wren Propp, *Albuquerque Journal*; Patricia Barry, *AARP Bulletin*; Lars Tulin, *DI*; James Sams, *Chicago Maroon*; Al Franken, *Al Franken Show*; Joan Indiana Rigdon, *Washington Lawyer*; Spencer Rich, *Congress Daily*; Paul Harris, *Infinity Broadcasting*; Al Swanson, UPI; Agnes Shanley, *Pharmaceutical Manufacturing*; Ross Sneyd, Associated Press; John Gregg, *Valley News*; Darren Allen, *Rutland Herald*; Evelyn Pringle, *Independent Media TV*; Kitta MacPherson, *Star-Ledger*; Frederic Frommer, Associated Press; Joseph Straw, *Journal Register News Service*; Katarina Anderson, SR; Stefan Asberg, SVT; Fredrik Hed, *Lakemedelsvarlden*; Warren Wolfe and Dave Hage, *Star Tribune*; Gary Null, *The Gary Null Show*; Mary Morgan, *Ann Arbor News*; Stephanie Saul, *The New York Times*; Steve Maich, *Macleans*; Trudy Lieberman, *Columbia Journalism Review*.

Also, I am indebted to those who helped me keep my job for as long as I did and supported me through very difficult times. Congressman Rahm Emanuel (D-IL), Congressman Dan Burton (R-IN), Congressman Sherrod Brown (D-OH), Congresswoman Rosa DeLauro (D-CT), Congressman James Langevin (D-RI), Congressman Marion Berry (D-AR), and Congressman Bernie Sanders (I-VT) who, collectively, sent a letter to Pfizer CEO Hank McKinnell and Pfizer's board of directors asking them to halt Pfizer's intimidation efforts. Senator Byron Dorgan (D-ND) should receive a particular thank you after he called Pfizer directly to assist me and Senator Edward Kennedy (D-MA), for inviting me to testify before the United States Senate. Others who were supportive were Senate Minority Leader Tom Daschle (D-SD), Senator Olympia Snowe (R-ME), Senator Debbie Stabenow (D-MI), Congressman Gil Gutknecht, (R-MN), Congresswoman Jo Ann Emerson (R-MO), and Congresswoman Anne Northup (R-KY).

This manuscript would never have been printed without the review and approval of my talented employment lawyer Jon Green or without the help of the experienced media lawyer Steven Schechter, author of *The Copyright Permission and Libel Handbook.*

Most of all I would like to thank my gutsy publisher, Richard Nash, who is a true visionary, unafraid of any size opponent, and to also thank my wife Tina, who has stood by my side, unwavering, no matter what happened to us. Thank you Richard and Tina, I couldn't have done this without you.

Notes

Chapter 1

1. Interview: Fred Hassan, President and Chief Executive Officer of Pharmacia Corporation, "Making Culture a Strategic Asset," *Outlook Journal,* January 2001.
2. Ibid.
3. Scripts and slides used for a conference call on July 17, 2002. Filed by Pfizer Inc., pursuant to Rule 425, with the SEC July 17, 2002.
4. Scott-Levin data 2002, "Top Ten U.S. Pharmaceutical Companies Ranked by U.S. Sales." Filed by Pfizer Inc., pursuant to Rule 425, with the SEC July 23, 2002.
5. Cafépharma message board for Pfizer.
6. Jamie Reidy, *Hard Sell: The Evolution of a Viagra Salesman.*
7. Transcript, global employee broadcast, Pharmacia Corporation, July 15, 2002.
8. Pfizer 10-Q, first quarter 2004.
9. Amy Barrett, "Pfizer's Funk," *Business Week*, February 28, 2005, cover story.
10. Hank McKinnell, "Message from Pfizer Chairman & CEO Hank McKinnell," August 12, 2002.

Chapter 2

1. Pfizer job offer letter from Harry Otter to Isadora Pelozzi, December 19, 2002.
2. E-mail from Isadora Pelozzi to Harry Otter, and others, January 2, 2003.
3. Ibid, January 16, 2003.
4. Pfizer December 31, 2003 and December 31, 2004 sales reports.
5. Amended and restated employment agreements for Fred Hassan and his direct reports, filed with the SEC on December 20, 2002, by Pharmacia Corp., DE.
6. PHA_NEWS, "Policy on Employment References Outlined," March 14, 2003.
7. Peter Rost, e-mail to Adrian Hoffman, and others, March 14, 2003.

Chapter 3

1. Manager Job Loss Notification Meeting Guide. For Pfizer (legacy Pharmacia) Employees.
2. Ibid.
3. Ibid.

Chapter 4

1. Darren McAllister, "Growth Hormone in Aging Patients," May 21, 2001.
2. The federal health care Anti-Kickback statute, 42 U.S.C. §1320a-7b(b) prohibits any person or entity from making or accepting payment to induce or reward any person for referring, recommending or arranging for the purchase of any item for which payment may be made under a federally-funded health care program.

3. Adult GHD Sales & Marketing Strategy Presentation, February 27, 2002.

4. Ibid.

5. Pfizer December 31, 2003 sales report.

6. Meeting Pfizer, New York, October 28, 2002.

7. Wyler Jennings, e-mail to Peter Rost, November 13, 2002.

8. Gertrude Hawk, e-mail to Peter Rost, September 17, 2002.

9. Letter from Professors Michael B. Ranke, Edinburgh; Kerstin Albertsson-Wikland, Gothenburg; Pierre Chatelain, Lyon; David Antony Price, Manchester; Roger Abs, Antwerp; Bengt-Ake Bengtsson, Gothenburg; Ulla-Feldt-Rasmussen, Copenhagen; John P. Monson, London to Mr. Fred Hassan, August 21, 2000.

10. Professor Bengt-Ake Bengtsson, e-mail to Peter Rost, September 12, 2003.

Chapter 5

1. David Cay Johnston, Melody Petersen, "Whistle-Blower Accuses Wyeth of Tax Dodges," *New York Times*, January 17, 2003.

2. Paul Beckett and Jathon Sapsford, "Wyeth Ex-Officer's Suit Revisits Foreign Tax Issues," *The Wall Street Journal*, January 20, 2003.

3. Securities and Exchange Commission subpoena to Peter Rost, February 12, 2003.

4. Wyler Jennings, e-mail to Peter Rost, January 17, 2003.

5. Peter Rost, e-mail to Wyler Jennings, January 21, 2003.

6. Bosse Pettersson, "Pharmacia CEO in U.S. scandal," *Veckans Affärer*, February 3, 2003.

7. Professor Bengt-Ake Bengtsson, e-mail to Fred Hassan, January 24, 2003.

8. Wyler Jennings, e-mail to Peter Rost, February 2, 2003.

9. Letter from Pharmacia's General Counsel to Peter Rost, February 3, 2003.

Chapter 6

1. Case Report, Case 2003-02-00003 Corporate, Pharmacia Corporate Security, February 6, 2003.
2. Ibid.
3. Pfizer lawyer, e-mail to Pharmacia, February 3, 2003.
4. E-mail from recruiter to Peter Rost, March 4, 2003.
5. "Interview Report for Peter Rost, M.D.," by Strawn, Arnold Leech & Ashpitz, Inc., April 19, 2001.

Chapter 7

1. Peter Rost, e-mail to Pharmacia's General Counsel, and others, February 4, 2003.
2. Ronald Chapman, e-mail to Pharmacia's General Counsel, March 2, 2003.
3. Pharmacia's General Counsel, e-mail to Ronald Chapman, March 3, 2003.
4. Peter Rost, e-mail to Ronald Chapman, March 13, 2003.
5. "Top Products Report," US Market Company Including GBM US, Sales & EBIT – April 2003 FCST.
6. Fred Hassan, e-mail to Peter Rost, March 31, 2003.
7. "Release Agreement," Pharmacia Corporation, the Separation Coordinating Office.
8. Peter Rost, e-mail to endocrine care department, April 17, 2003.
9. Peter Rost, e-mail to endocrine care department, April 17, 2003.
10. Wyler Jennings, e-mail to Peter Rost, and others, April 17, 2003.
11. Peter Rost, e-mail to Ronald Chapman, and others, April 30, 2003.
12. Peter Rost, e-mail to Lorenzo Ellenberg, May 22, 2003.

13. Lorenzo Ellenberg, e-mail to Peter Rost, and others, May 29, 2003.
14. Ronald Chapman, letter to Peter Rost, May 28, 2003.
15. Tamar Lewin, "Families Sue Pfizer on Test of Antibiotics," *New York Times*, August 30, 2001.
16. Pfizer Annual Report 2003.
17. http://www.oig.hhs.gov/fraud/cia/

Chapter 8

1. "Results of the 2001 Pfizer Values Survey; a Report to Colleagues."
2. Peter Rost, e-mail to Hank McKinnell and Ronald Chapman, August 18, 2003.
3. Hank McKinnell, e-mail to Peter Rost and Ronald Chapman, August 18, 2003.
4. Ronald Chapman, e-mail to Peter Rost, August 18, 2003.
5. Arthur Richardson, e-mail to Peter Rost, and others, August 20, 2003.
6. Arthur Richardson, e-mail to Peter Rost, August 21, and others, 2003.
7. Arthur Richardson, phone call to Peter Rost on November 11, 2003.
8. Leslie Wayne, "Boeing Chief Is Ousted after Admitting Affair," *New York Times*, March 8, 2005.
9. Stanley Holmes, "The Affair that Grounded Stonecipher," *Business Week*, March 8, 2005.
10. "2004 Global Colleagues Survey Results; Listening to the Voice of Pfizer Colleagues."

Chapter 9

1. Elizabeth Olson, "Big Puerto Rico Bank Settles U.S. Money Laundering Case," *New York Times*, January 17, 2003.

2. Jim Hopkins and Edward Iwata, "WorldCom directors' credibility doubted," *USA Today*, June 10, 2003.

3. Bruce Meyerson, "WorldCom Execs To Pay $18M," Associated Press, January 7, 2005.

4. Jerry Useem, "12 Piggy Offenders" *Fortune*, April 14, 2003.

5. Jerry Useem, "Have They No Shame?" *Fortune*, April 14, 2003.

6. Lu Chia-ying, "Wyeth executive falls to his death from apartment," *Taiwan News*, February 21, 2005.

Chapter 10

1. Ed Silverman, "Wyeth and former executive settle suit," *Star-Ledger*, October 31, 2003.

2. Dabeaka2, "Re: Whistleblower lawsuit settled," Yahoo! Message Boards: WYE, Msg: 37619, November 1, 2003.

3. Wyler Jennings, e-mail to Peter Rost, February 2, 2003.

4. Peter Rost, e-mail to Arthur Richardson, September 19, 2003.

5. Arthur Richardson, e-mail to Peter Rost, and others, September 23, 2003.

6. Peter Rost, note to file, September 29, 2003.

7. Peter Rost, note to file, November 11, 2003.

8. Peter Rost, note to file, June 10, 2004.

Chapter 11

1. Peter Rost, e-mail to Darren McAllister, July 1, 2002.

2. A48) in Pfizer 8-K Submission, Current report, items 12 and 7; filed with the SEC January 22, 2004.

3. Associated Press, "Pharmacia Inventory Cuts Pfizer Earnings," June 17, 2003.

Chapter 12

1. Tom Reason, "The Untouchables," *CFO Magazine*, March 1, 2003.
2. U.S. Code, Title 18, section 1513.
3. Peter Rost, e-mail to Pamela Berlin, Wyler Jennings, Robert Chapman, Lorenzo Ellenberg, February 16, 2004.
4. Pamela Berlin, e-mail to P. Rost and others, Feb. 27, 2004.

Chapter 13

1. Tom Reason, "The Untouchables," *CFO Magazine*, March 1, 2003.
2. The Compliance Partners, "Retaliation."
3. "A Firm-by-Firm Sampling of Billing Rates Nationwide," Law.com, 2002 Survey by the *National Law Journal.*
4. Peter Rost, e-mail to Gideon Braxton, Ronald Chapman, and others, March 12, 2004.
5. Pamela Berlin, e-mail to Peter Rost and others, March 25, 2004.
6. Peter Rost, e-mail to Pamela Berlin, Hank McKinnell, and others, March 31, 2004.

Chapter 14

1. Consultant name withheld, Company name withheld, May 28, 2004.
2. Darren, McAllister, "Session I: Assessment and Coaching, Year 2002," November 18, 2002.
3. Pamela Berlin, e-mail to Peter Rost and others, March 25, 2004.
4. Jon Green, letter to Pamela Berlin, April 15, 2004.
5. Tolling agreement between Peter Rost and Pfizer, April 20, 2004.

Chapter 15

1. Rita Rubin, "Prescription for reform?" *USA Today*, September 13, 2004.
2. David Schwab, "Drug exec renews calls for import," *Star-Ledger*, September 11, 2004.
3. Theresa Agovino, "Pfizer Exec Support Drug Importation," Associated Press, September 10, 2004.
4. Tim Craig, "Surprise Support for Drug Importing," *Washington Post*, September 14, 2004.
5. Peter Rost, e-mail to Ronald Chapman, and others, September 9, 2004.

Chapter 17

1. Scott Hensley, "Fight to Legalize Drug Imports Has Unlikely Ally," *Wall Street Journal*, September 22, 2004.
2. U.S. Code, Title 18, section 1512.
3. U.S. Code, Title 18, section 1515.
4. Congressman Rahm Emanuel, Press Release, September 23, 2004.
5. David Schwab, "Stirring up controversy," *Star-Ledger*, September 23, 2004.
6. Robert Pear, "Insider Challenges Drug Industry on Imports," *New York Times*, September 24, 2004.
7. Ibid.
8. Ibid.
9. Kevin Freking, "Allow reimported drugs, Pfizer exec urges," *Arkansas Democrat-Gazette*, September 24, 2004.
10. Robert Pear, "Insider Challenges Drug Industry on Imports," *New York Times*, September 24, 2004.
11. Kristen Hallam, "Pfizer Executive Rost Backs Vote on Drug-Import Bill," Bloomberg News, September 23, 2004.

12. Editorial, "Drug imports could be safe," *Wilmington Star*, September 26, 2004.

13. Editorial, "Dr. Frist, tear down this death wall!" *Chattanooga Times Free Press*, September 25, 2004.

Chapter 18

1. http://www.house.gov/apps/list/press/il05_emanuel/ rost_pfizer_letter.pdf

2. Tim Craig, "Pfizer Lawyers Grill Dissenting Executive," *Washington Post*, October 1, 2004.

3. Peter Rost, e-mail to Carl Finkelberg, October 1, 2004.

4. Peter Rost, e-mail to Harry Otter and Ivana Fokker, October 1, 2004.

5. Peter Rost, e-mail to Clark Finkelberg, copy to NY and NJ Justice Department, October 4, 2004.

6. Harry Otter, e-mail to Peter Rost, October 12, 2004.

7. Ivana Fokker, e-mail to Peter Rost, October 8, 2004.

8. Peter Rost, e-mail to Harry Otter and Ivana Fokker, October 14, 2004.

Chapter 19

1. Senator Chuck Grassley, Remarks Before the Consumer Federation of America, March 10, 2005.

2. U.S. Department of Justice, press release, October 3, 2001.

3. FDA, press release, November 2, 1999.

4. U.S. Department of Justice, press release, November 10, 2003.

5. U.S. Department of Justice, press release, June 20, 2003.

6. U.S. Department of Justice, press release, October 28, 2002.

7. U.S. Department of Justice, press release, May 13, 2004.

8. The False Claims Act Legal Center; Top 20 Cases.

9. The Department of Health and Human Services and The

U.S. Department of Justice Health Care Fraud and Abuse Control Program Annual Report For FY 2003. Denise Lavoie, "Bayer AG, GlaxoSmithKline agree to settle alleged Medicaid overcharges," Associated Press, April 17, 2003.

10. "Bayer Pleads Guilty In Medicaid Fraud Case," Corporate Crime Reporter, April 21, 2003.

11. U.S. Department of Justice, press release, January 23, 2001.

12. Al Rauch, an analyst at A.G. Edwards, according to Matthew Herper, "Vioxx Liability to Force Biotechs To Merge," *Forbes*, September 14, 2005. Friedman, Billings, Ramsey & Co, "Merck's Vioxx bill could hit $50 billion," CNN Money, August 22, 2005.

13. Alex Berenson, "Merck Jury Adds $9 Million in Damages," *New York Times*, April 12, 2006.

14. Class Action Reporter, January 21, 2004, Vol. 6, No. 14.

15. Robert Steyer, "Merck Disputes IRS Ruling," TheStreet.com, May 10, 2004.

16. Heather Tomlinson, "Glaxo faces $7.8bn US tax bill," *The Guardian*, January 27, 2005.

17. Ibid.

18. Jill Treanor and Julia Finch, "Directors' gains stir revolt by investors," *The Guardian*, July 31, 2003. Neil Collins, "Why I'm worth it, by the £22m Glaxo 'fat cat'," *The Telegraph*, May 21, 2003.

19. U.S. Department of Justice, press release, February 24, 1997.

20. Wisconsin U.S. Department of Justice, press release, May 20, 2003.

21. Sylvia Pfeifer, "Garnier comes out fighting," *The Telegraph*, June 6, 2004.

22. Stephen Evans, "A Spitzer in the eye for Glaxo," BBC News, June 4, 2004.

23. Sylvia Pfeifer, "Garnier comes out fighting," *The Telegraph*, June 6, 2004.

24. Thomas Ginsberg, "Glaxo shares rise on strong 1st-quarter profits," *Philadelphia Inquirer*, April 28, 2005.

25. U.S. Department of Justice, press release, September 20, 2005.

26. New Jersey Department of Justice, press release, June 15, 2005.

27. Paul Davies, Joann S. Lublin and Barbara Martinez, "Bristol-Myers Ex-Officials Are Indicted," *Wall Street Journal*, June 16, 2005.

28. Ibid.

29. FDA Talk Paper, October 3, 2000.

30. Robert Steyer, "Sizing Up the Vioxx Effect at Merck," TheStreet.com, August 17, 2005.

31. FDA, press release, May 17, 2002.

32. U.S. Department of Justice, press release, July 30, 2004.

33. U.S. Department of Justice, press release, October 17, 2005.

34. U.S. Department of Justice, press release, December 21, 2005.

35. Julie Schmit, "Drugmaker admitted fraud, but sales flourish," *USA Today*, August 16, 2004.

36. Neil Weinberg, "The Dark Side of Whistleblowing," *Forbes*, March 14, 2005.

Chapter 20

1. Gardiner Harris and Alex Berenson, "10 Voters on Panel Backing Pain Pills Had Industry Ties," *New York Times*, February 25, 2005.

2. Ibid.

3. Ibid.

4. Ibid.

5. Ibid.

6. Ibid.

7. Kaiser Family Foundation, news release, February 25, 2005.
8. Health Talk, "Most FDA Scientists Lack Confidence In Agency," December 16, 2004.
9. Marc Kaufmann, "Many FDA Scientists Had Drug Concerns, 2002 Survey Shows," *Washington Post*, December 16, 2004.
10. Paul Recer, "Lawmakers Press FDA on Whistleblower," Associated Press, December 11, 2004.

Chapter 21

1. Arthur Richardson, e-mail to Pfizer personnel, Aug. 13, 2004.
2. Peter Rost, e-mail to Eliot Spitzer, August 17, 2004.
3. Peter Drago, letter to Peter Rost, August 31, 2004 and Joe Baker, e-mail to Peter Rost, October 13, 2004.
4. Meeting with Rose Firestein, November 15, 2004.
5. Peter Rost, e-mail to Christopher Christie, October 26, 2004.

Chapter 22

1. Ben Hirschler, "Third-quarter results highlight big pharma's ills," Reuters, October 22, 2004.
2. Peter Rost, "Medicines without Borders," *New York Times*, October 30, 2004.
3. "Top 25 Most E-Mailed Articles," *New York Times*, October 30, 2004, 8:44 P.M.
4. Wren Propp, "Doctors Close Door On Pfizer," *Albuquerque Journal*, October 29, 2004.
5. Wren Propp, e-mail to Peter Rost, October 29, 2004.
6. Wren Propp, "Pfizer Exec Thankful for Doctors' Boycott," *Albuquerque Journal*, October 30, 2004.
7. Peter Rost, "Big Pharma's Dirty Little Secret," *Los Angeles Times*, December 26, 2004.

Chapter 23

1. HHS Task Force on Drug Importation, Report on Prescription Drug Importation, December 2004.
2. Jennifer Corbett Dooren, "HHS Report: Drug Imports Likely Won't Save Money," Dow Jones Newswires, December 21, 2004.
3. *Indianapolis Star*, December 22, 2004.
4. *Baltimore Sun*, December 22, 2004.
5. Jennifer Corbett Dooren, "Bush Panel Sees Scant Savings in Drug Imports," *The Wall Street Journal*, December 22, 2004.
6. HHS Task Force on Drug Importation, Report on Prescription Drug Importation, Figure7.2.

Chapter 24

1. http://www.cbsnews.com/stories/2005/06/03/60minutes/main699606_page3.shtml
2. Ibid.
3. Jim Edwards, "Marketing Exec Feels Heat At Pfizer" *Brandweek*, June 7, 2005.
4. Jim Edwards, "Rost Finds Pfizer Privileges Restored" *Brandweek*, June 8, 2005.
5. Alex Berenson, "At Pfizer, the Isolation Increases for a Whistle-Blower," *New York Times*, June 8, 2005.
6. Theresa Agovino, "Pfizer exec says company froze him out," Associated Press, June 7, 2005.
7. Alex Berenson, "At Pfizer, the Isolation Increases for a Whistle-Blower," *New York Times*, June 8, 2005.
8. Peter Rost, e-mail to Pfizer IT, June 7, 2005.
9. Peter Rost, e-mail to Ronald Chapman and Pfizer PR, June 13, 2005.
10. Stewart Bolling, letter to Jon Green, June 17, 2005.

11. Dorothy Lippenwurst, e-mail to Peter Rost, July 8, 2005.
12. Alex Berenson, "At Pfizer, the Isolation Increases for a Whistle-Blower," *New York Times*, June 8, 2005.

Chapter 25

1. Jim Edwards, "Pfizer Fable takes Another Strange Twist," *Brandweek*, July 7, 2005.
2. Ed Silverman, "Another stinger from Pfizer's gadfly," *Star-Ledger*, July 21, 2005.
3. John Kador, e-mail to Peter Rost, July 5, 2005.

Chapter 26

1. For additional reading on this topic, see Trudy Lieberman, "Bitter Pill," *Columbia Journalism Review*, July-August 2005.
2. Jim Drinkard, "Drugmakers go furthest to sway Congress," *USA Today*, April 25, 2005.
3. Alex Berenson, "Evidence in Vioxx Suits Shows Intervention by Merck Officials," *New York Times*, April 24, 2005.
4. Senator Herb Kohl, news release, November 24, 2003.
5. Valerie Reitman, "Medicare Drug Plans Often Not the Bargain Some Expect," *Los Angeles Times*, April 18, 2006.

Afterword

1. Cary O'Reilly and John Lauerman, "Pfizer Fires Marketing VP Rost After U.S. Spurns Suit," Bloomberg News, December 1, 2005.
2. Danylo Hawaleshka, "Big money, big fines—it's all hormonal," Macleans, February 23, 2006.
3. Gilbert Ross, M.D., "Whiny Whistleblower of the Year Award," American Council on Science and Health, December 30, 2005.

4. http://www.cspinet.org/integrity/nonprofits/american_council_on_science_and_health.html

5. Bill Hogan, "Paging Dr. Ross," Mother Jones, November/December 2005 issue.

6. http://www.house.gov/apps/list/press/il05_emanuel/rost_pfizer_letter.pdf

7. http://www.greensavits.com/Dec1st2005.pdf

8. http://www.patientrecruitment.com/pdf/In%20the%20Courts% 20Nigerian%20Suit %20Against%20Pfizer%2008-30-01.pdf

9. Alex Berenson, "Pfizer Fires a Vice President Who Criticized the Company's Sales Practices," New York Times, December 2, 2005.

10. http://www.greensavits.com/May28&Jun9,2003.pdf

11. http://www.oig.hhs.gov/fraud/cia/agreements/pfizer_5_11_2004.pdf

12. http://www.usdoj.gov/opa/pr/2002/October/02_civ_622.htm
http://www.usdoj.gov/opa/pr/2004/May/04_civ_322.htm

13. http://www.dol.gov/

14. http://www.economist.com/finance/displayStory.cfm?story_id=4223595

15. http://www.thinkandask.com/news/jobs.html

16. NJ Department of Labor Notice to Claimant of Benefit Determination BC-3C (R-10-99)

17. http://aspe.hhs.gov/poverty/06poverty.shtml

18. http://scooter.gnn.tv/hcadlincs/3297/At_Pfizer_the_Isolation_Increases _for_a_Whistle_Blower

19. Cobra Fact Sheet, January 6, 2006

20. http://www.sec.gov/Archives/edgar/data/78003/000093041306001378/ c39174_pre14a.htm

21. Ibid.

22. http://www.sec.gov/Archives/edgar/data/78003/000007800305000277/ q3-05pfe1.htm

23. http://www.forbes.com/2005/03/10/0310autofacescan06.html

24. Stephen Labaton, "S.E.C. to Require More Disclosure Of Executive Pay," New York Times, January 18, 2006.

25. http://www.cbpp.org/9-1-05mw.htm

26. http://www.usatoday.com/money/industries/health/drugs/2005-04-25-drug-lobby-cover_x.htm

27. http://open.imshealth.com/IMSinclude/i_article_20040929.asp

28. http://www.house.gov/stupak/issues_prescription.shtml

29. http://www.nytimes.com/2006/01/21/politics/21drug.html

30. http://www.google.com/search?sourceid=gd&hl=en&oe=UTF-8&q=define%3Akleptocracy&sa=N&tab=xw